RACHAEL RAY

TOP 30

30-MINUTE MEALS

GUY
food

♦

Compilation copyright © 2005 Rachael Ray

Cover photograph of Rachael Ray copyright © 2004 Jean-Claude Dhien

All recipes in this book are reprinted from previously published books by Rachael Ray, namely, *30-Minute Meals*, *The Open House Cookbook*, *Comfort Foods*, *Veggie Meals*, *30-Minute Meals 2*, *Get Togethers*, and *Cooking 'Round the Clock*.

Published by:
Lake Isle Press, Inc.
16 West 32nd Street, Suite 10-B
New York, NY 10001
(212) 273-0796
E-mail: lakeisle@earthlink.net

Distributed to the trade by:
National Book Network (NBN), Inc.
4501 Forbes Boulevard, Suite 200
Lanham, MD 20706
1 (800) 462-6420
www.nbnbooks.com

Library of Congress Control Number: 2005929074

ISBN: 1-891105-21-3

Food photography copyright © 2005 Tina Rupp

Book and cover design: Ellen Swandiak

This book is available at special sales discounts for bulk purchases as premiums or special editions, including personalized covers. For more information, contact the publisher at (212) 273-0796 or by e-mail, lakeisle@earthlink.net

First Edition

Printed in China

10 9 8

For all the hungry men

RACHAEL RAY

TOP 30

30-MINUTE MEALS

This book is for guys who love to cook and eat!
Simple, hearty meals packed with big flavors are
on the menu. Sage Veal Chops, Manly Manny's
Chili, and You-Won't-Be-Single-For-Long Vodka
Cream Pasta are just a sampling of the recipes I've
chosen. No fuss; only easy-to-find ingredients.
Perfect for watching sports, hanging out with
friends, and impressing a date. A man who cooks
is hot! The dishes can wait 'til morning…

RACHAEL RAY

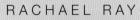

30-MINUTE MEALS

DON'T MEASURE WITH INSTRUMENTS, USE YOUR HANDS.

You're not baking or conducting experiments for the government—just feel your way through.

HOW TO MEASURE RACHAEL'S WAY:

A HANDFUL
about 3 tablespoons

◆

A PALMFUL
about 2 tablespoons

◆

HALF A PALMFUL
you do the math

◆

A PINCH
about 1/4 teaspoon

◆

A FEW GOOD PINCHES
about 1 teaspoon

◆

ONCE AROUND THE PAN
about 1 tablespoon of liquid

◆

TWICE AROUND THE PAN
more math: about 2 tablespoons,
3 or 4 would be 1/4 cup

◆

RACHAEL RAY

TOP 30

30-MINUTE MEALS

OUTSIDE-IN
BACON CHEESEBURGERS *with*
GREEN ONION MAYO

BEEFSTEAK TOMATO &
VIDALIA ONION SALAD
with STEAK SAUCE DRESSING

makes 6 servings

GUY*food*

Outside-In
BACON CHEESEBURGERS
with Green Onion Mayo

6 slices bacon, chopped

4 scallions, cleaned and trimmed

Extra-virgin olive oil, for drizzling

1 & 3/4 pounds ground beef sirloin

1 & 1/2 tablespoons Worcestershire sauce

1 & 1/2 tablespoons Montreal Steak Seasoning by
  McCormick, or coarse salt and fresh black pepper

3/4 pound extra-sharp white cheddar cheese, crumbled

1 cup mayonnaise or reduced-fat mayonnaise

1 teaspoon ground cumin

Salt and freshly ground black pepper

6 crusty Kaiser rolls, split

6 leaves crisp romaine lettuce

Preheat grill pan over high heat.

In a medium pan, brown bacon and drain on a paper towel–lined plate.

Brush scallions with a little evoo and grill on hot grill pan 2 or 3 minutes on each side. Remove from heat to cool.

Combine ground beef with Worcestershire and steak seasoning or salt and pepper. Divide meat into 6 equal parts. Combine cheese crumbles and cooked bacon. Take a portion of the ground meat in your hand and make a well in the center. Pile in cheese and bacon, then carefully form the burger around the filling. Make sure the fillings are completely covered with meat. When all 6 patties are formed, drizzle burgers with evoo and place on hot grill pan. Cook 2 minutes on each side over high heat, reduce heat to medium-low and cook burgers 7 or 8 minutes longer, turning occasionally. Do not press down on burgers as they cook. Transfer to a plate and let them rest 5 minutes before serving.

Make the mayonnaise: Chop cooled, grilled green onions and add to a food processor. Add mayonnaise and cumin and pulse-grind together. Season with salt and pepper to taste.

Place burgers on crusty buns and top with crisp lettuce leaves and a slather of green onion mayonnaise.

"Heads up: read through a recipe before you start cooking.**"**

BEEFSTEAK TOMATO & VIDALIA ONION SALAD *with*
Steak Sauce Dressing

1/4 cup red wine vinegar

3 rounded tablespoons brown sugar

1 tablespoon Worcestershire sauce

1 teaspoon coarse black pepper

1 cup canned tomato sauce

2 tablespoons extra-virgin olive oil

4 beefsteak tomatoes, sliced 1/2-inch thick

1 large Vidalia onion, peeled and cut into 1/2-inch thick rings

Salt, to taste

3 tablespoons chopped parsley, for garnish

Make the dressing: In a small saucepan over moderate heat combine vinegar, sugar, Worcestershire, and pepper. Allow sugar to dissolve and liquids to come to a bubble. Remove sauce from heat and whisk in tomato sauce, then evoo. Serve warm or chilled.

Arrange sliced tomatoes and onions on a serving platter. Season with salt. Pour dressing over the tomatoes and onions and garnish with chopped parsley.

RACHAEL RAY

30-MINUTE MEALS

MANLY MANNY'S CHILI

SERVE *with* CORN CHIPS

makes 6 servings

Manly Manny's CHILI

2 tablespoons corn or vegetable oil

1 large onion, chopped fine

4 cloves garlic, minced

1 & 1/2 pounds ground sirloin, 90% lean

Montreal Steak Seasoning or salt and pepper, to taste

1/2 bottle beer (6 ounces)

1 can (14 ounces) beef broth

1 can (6 ounces) tomato paste

1 & 1/2 tablespoons dark chili powder

1 tablespoon ground cumin

2 ounces smoky barbecue sauce (2 glugs)

2 ounces hot sauce (about 3 tablespoons)

6 ounces shredded smoked cheddar cheese

Chopped raw onions (optional)

Heat oil in a deep pot over medium-high heat. Add onions and garlic; sauté 3 to 5 minutes, stirring frequently. Add beef and brown, another 3 to 5 minutes. Season lightly with Montreal seasoning or salt and pepper. Add beer and let it reduce by half.

Stir in broth, paste, chili powder, cumin, barbecue sauce, and hot sauce. Reduce heat to medium low and simmer 10 minutes. Top with cheddar and onions, if using. Serve with corn chips.

RACHAEL RAY

TOP 30

30-MINUTE MEALS

BLACKENED CHICKEN
PIZZA *with*
YELLOW TOMATO SALSA

SERVE *with* GREEN SALAD

makes 2 servings

BLACKENED CHICKEN PIZZA
with Yellow Tomato Salsa

1 tablespoon Montreal Steak Seasoning by McCormick

1 teaspoon sweet paprika

1 teaspoon chili powder

1/2 teaspoon cayenne pepper or a few drops hot sauce

1/2 to 3/4 pound chicken breast, sliced thin

1 tablespoon vegetable oil

All-purpose flour or corn meal, for dusting

1 store-bought pizza dough

1/2 pound brick reduced-fat cheese with jalapeño
   pepper, such as Cabot brand

2 small yellow tomatoes, seeded and chopped

1/4 cup chopped red onion

1 jalapeño pepper, seeded and finely chopped

2 tablespoons cilantro (optional)

2 tablespoons fresh thyme leaves

1 clove garlic, cracked away from skins

Salt, to taste

The zest and juice of 1/2 lime

Preheat oven to 450°F.

Heat a large, heavy skillet over very high heat. Combine grill seasoning, paprika, chili powder, and cayenne pepper on a plate. Press chicken slices into seasoning on one side. Add oil to screaming hot pan and cook chicken 2 minutes on each side. Remove chicken from skillet and chop.

Sprinkle a little flour or corn meal on a pizza pan or cookie sheet and stretch out pizza dough on pan. Shred reduced-fat cheese.

Make the salsa: Combine tomatoes, onion, jalapeño, cilantro (if using), and thyme. Make a garlic paste by chopping garlic then adding a generous pinch of salt and mashing it together with the flat of the knife. Add garlic paste to salsa. Add lime zest and juice and mix salsa well.

Scatter chicken, salsa, and cheese over pizza dough, working to the edges. Bake until crisp and bubbly-brown on top, 12 to 15 minutes. Serve with a green salad, dressed in lime juice, olive oil, salt, and pepper.

RACHAEL RAY

TOP
30

30-MINUTE MEALS

GRILLED
MAHI-MAHI FILLETS

ASPARAGUS
with ORANGE AND SESAME

makes 4 servings

Grilled **MAHI-MAHI** Fillets

4 portions mahi-mahi fillets (6 to 8 ounces each)

Salt and freshly ground black pepper, to taste

The juice of 2 limes

3 tablespoons Tamari dark soy sauce

2 inches fresh gingerroot, grated (1 & 1/2 tablespoons)

1 tablespoon vegetable or canola oil

20 blades fresh chives, chopped or 3 scallions, thinly
    sliced, for garnish

Preheat grill pan over medium-high to high heat. Season
mahi-mahi fillets with salt and pepper. Combine lime
juice, dark soy, ginger, and a little vegetable or canola oil
in a shallow dish. Turn fish in the citrus-soy marinade and
let it "hang out" for 10 minutes. Grill 4 to 5 minutes per
side or until fish is firm and opaque.

"Relax! You're not racing the clock, you're only making dinner.**"**

ASPARAGUS
with Orange and Sesame

2 navel oranges
1 inch fresh gingerroot, peeled
Salt
1 to 1 & 3/4 pounds thin asparagus spears, trimmed
2 tablespoons toasted sesame seeds

Cut the ends off two navel oranges and stand them upright on a cutting board. Remove skins in strips using a sharp knife to cut down from the top of the orange. Reserve the peels of 1 orange. When peeled and trimmed, slice into 1/4-inch rounds, and set aside.

In a skillet with cover, bring 1-inch of water to a boil with the peels of 1 orange and the gingerroot. When the water boils, add a healthy pinch of salt and asparagus spears. Simmer 3 to 5 minutes until just tender, then drain. Assemble a few spears on each dinner plate, crisscrossing the spears and orange slices. Finish with a sprinkle of sesame seeds and top with 1 portion of grilled mahi mahi. Garnish plates with chopped chives and serve.

RACHAEL RAY

TOP 30

30-MINUTE MEALS

TRIPLE-A PASTA: SPINACH PASTA *with* ASPARAGUS, ARTICHOKE, AND ARUGULA

SERVE *with* CRUSTY BREAD *and* FRESH SLICED MELON

Serves 4

TRIPLE-A PASTA:
Spinach Pasta *with* Asparagus, Artichoke, and Arugula

12 ounces spinach fettuccine, dried or fresh, cooked until al dente

Extra-virgin olive oil, a drizzle

1 tablespoon butter

2 tablespoons extra-virgin olive oil

1 large or 2 medium shallots, finely chopped

1/2 cup white wine

1 pound thin fresh asparagus spears, trimmed and cut on angle into bite-size pieces

1 cup broth, chicken or vegetable

1 can (14 ounces) artichoke hearts in water, drained and chopped

24 leaves fresh arugula, torn or coarsely chopped

2 tablespoons zest from 1 large lemon (grate skin, not the white part)

Coarse salt and black pepper, to taste

A handful chopped fresh flat-leaf parsley, to garnish

Drain pasta well and drizzle with oil to keep from sticking. Set aside.

Heat a large, deep skillet over medium heat. Add butter and olive oil to pan and heat until butter is melted. Add shallots and sauté, 3 minutes. Add wine and reduce liquid by half, about 2 minutes more. Add asparagus bits, cover, and cook, 3 or 4 minutes. Then uncover, adding broth and artichokes to pan. Heat artichokes through and add cooked pasta. Sprinkle in arugula. Toss ingredients until arugula wilts. Season with lemon zest, salt and pepper, and parsley, to taste.

Serve immediately with crusty bread. Fresh sliced melon makes a simple and wonderful accompaniment to this meal.

RACHAEL RAY

30-MINUTE MEALS

VEAL SCALOPPINI
with WINE, MUSHROOMS, AND GREEN OLIVES

SERVE *with* GREEN SALAD

makes 4 servings

VEAL SCALOPPINI *with* Wine, Mushrooms, and Green Olives

3/4 pound linguini

Salt and freshly ground black pepper, to taste

1/4 cup extra-virgin olive oil, plus some for drizzling

3 slices pancetta or bacon, chopped

1 small onion, chopped

16 crimini or button mushrooms, chopped

1 pound veal scaloppini, cut into 1-inch strips

2 cloves garlic, smashed

1 cup dry white wine

16 pitted, large green olives, coarsely chopped

A handful chopped, fresh flat-leaf Italian parsley

1 tablespoon butter, cut into pieces

1/3 cup grated Parmigiano Reggiano or Romano
cheese (a couple handfuls)

"If you keep those pots rocking, your date will keep on knocking…at your door.**"**

In a big pot, bring water to boil, add salt, and cook linguini 8 minutes, to al dente.

Preheat a large heavy skillet over medium to medium-high heat. Add 1 tablespoon olive oil and the pancetta or bacon. Cook 1 to 2 minutes, then add onions and cook, another 2 to 3 minutes. Add mushrooms and cook, another 3 to 5 minutes.

While vegetables are cooking, season veal strips with salt and pepper. To a second skillet preheated over medium-high heat, add 1 & 1/2 tablespoons olive oil and 1 clove smashed garlic. Quick-fry half of the veal, searing each side of the strips, 1 to 2 minutes. Transfer to a plate and repeat with remaining veal. When done, add all of the veal and garlic to the onions and mushrooms, then add wine to the veal pan and scrape up the drippings. Cook wine down (and alcohol out), 2 to 3 minutes. Stir olives and parsley into veal and mushrooms, and serve on a bed of hot linguini tossed with a drizzle of olive oil, butter, and grated cheese. Serve with a green salad on the side.

RACHAEL RAY

TOP 30

30-MINUTE MEALS

TENDERLOIN STEAKS *with* GORGONZOLA

ROAST POTATOES *with* ROSEMARY

makes 4 servings

TENDERLOIN STEAKS
with Gorgonzola

4 beef tenderloin steaks, 1 & 1/2-inches thick, at room
  temperature
1 tablespoon extra-virgin olive oil
Salt and freshly ground black pepper, to taste
3/4 pound gorgonzola cheese
4 leaves fresh sage, thinly sliced

Place a large, flat griddle or skillet over high heat. When it
is hot, wipe the surface with oil using a pair of tongs and
a folded paper towel. Place steaks on hot pan and
caramelize, 2 minutes on each side. Reduce heat to
moderate and cook 4 to 5 minutes longer. Season with
salt and pepper.

Preheat broiler to high.

Arrange steaks on a baking sheet and top each with 3
ounces cheese. Place sheet 6 inches from broiler and
heat just long enough to melt the cheese. Remove from
the oven and top with sage. Let meat rest up to 5 minutes, allowing the juices to redistribute. Serve with roast
potatoes and a green salad.

ROAST POTATOES *with*
Rosemary

2 pounds small potatoes, baby Yukon gold or red skin

6 cloves garlic, cracked away from skin

2 to 3 tablespoons extra-virgin olive oil (just enough to coat potatoes)

2 tablespoons fresh rosemary leaves, chopped

Salt and freshly ground black pepper, to taste

Preheat oven to 500°F or highest setting.

Halve potatoes and place on a cookie sheet. Combine with garlic. Coat potatoes and garlic with oil and season with rosemary, salt, and pepper.

Place on lower rack of oven and roast 20 to 25 minutes, turning potatoes once after about 12 minutes. Continue roasting until golden and crisp at edges.

RACHAEL RAY

TOP 30

30-MINUTE MEALS

CRISPY CHICKEN CUTLETS
with BASIL-PARSLEY SAUCE

CHEESY RISI E BISI

makes 4 servings

CHEESY RISI E BISI

2 tablespoons extra-virgin olive oil
1 large clove garlic, finely chopped
1 small onion, finely chopped
1 cup Arborio rice
Salt and freshly ground black pepper, to taste
1/2 cup dry white wine
3 to 4 cups chicken broth
1/4 to 1/3 cup grated Parmigiano Reggiano cheese
2 tablespoons chopped fresh flat-leaf parsley
1 cup tiny frozen peas, thawed

Heat a medium skillet over medium-high heat. Add evoo, then garlic and onion and sauté, stirring constantly, 2 to 3 minutes. Add rice and a little salt and pepper. Cook another minute, then add wine and cook until wine is completely absorbed, 30 seconds. Add about 1 cup chicken broth and stir. Reduce heat to medium and cook until broth is absorbed, stirring often. Continue adding 1/2 cup broth each time liquid is completely absorbed, stirring all the while. Use as much broth as is needed to result in creamy, slightly chewy rice; takes about 22 minutes. Work on chicken while rice continues to cook; recipe follows.

When rice is cooked to desired consistency, remove from heat and stir in cheese, parsley, and peas.

CRISPY CHICKEN CUTLETS
with Basil-Parsley Sauce

2 pounds chicken cutlets

Salt and freshly ground black pepper

3 to 4 tablespoons all-purpose flour

1 cup Italian bread crumbs

1/3 to 1/2 cup grated Parmigiano Reggiano cheese

1 teaspoon crushed red pepper flakes

2 teaspoons poultry seasoning (half a palmful)

1 clove garlic

1 jar (3 ounces) pine nuts (pignoli)

The zest of 1 lemon (2 tablespoons)

2 eggs, beaten

Olive oil, for frying

1 plum tomato, seeded and finely chopped, for garnish

Sauce:

1 cup loosely packed basil leaves

1/2 cup loosely packed fresh flat-leaf parsley leaves

The juice of 1/2 lemon

Salt and freshly ground black pepper, to taste

1/4 cup extra-virgin olive oil

Season cutlets with salt and pepper on both sides. Place flour in a shallow dish and turn cutlets lightly in flour.

Combine bread crumbs, cheese, red pepper flakes, poultry seasoning, garlic, pine nuts, and lemon zest in a food processor and pulse-process to evenly mix. Transfer the mixture to a plate. Beat eggs in a separate shallow dish.

Heat a thin layer of oil, just enough to coat the bottom of the pan, in a large skillet over medium to medium-high heat. Coat cutlets in eggs then breading and place in hot oil. Cook cutlets in a single layer, in 2 batches if necessary, until breading is evenly browned and juices run clear, 3 or 4 minutes on each side. Remove to a plate and tent with aluminum foil to keep warm.

Make the sauce: Return food processor bowl to base and add basil, parsley, and lemon juice. Add a little salt and pepper. Turn processor on and stream in evoo until a loose paste forms.

Serve chicken cutlets with a generous topping of basil and parsley sauce. Garnish with tomato.

RACHAEL RAY

TOP 30

30-MINUTE MEALS

MOROCCAN RUB LAMB CHOPS

GARLIC CHICK PEAS *and* GREENS

makes 4 servings

Moroccan Rub LAMB CHOPS

12 loin lamb chops
1 tablespoon extra-virgin olive oil
1 tablespoon ground cumin
2 teaspoons ground turmeric
1 teaspoon sweet paprika
1 teaspoon coriander seeds
1 teaspoon garlic salt
1/2 teaspoon hot red pepper flakes
1 lemon, wedged

Preheat grill pan to high. Brush chops with a little olive oil.
Mix dry spices in a small container, cover and shake to
combine. Rub spice blend into the chops on both sides,
and grill 7 to 8 minutes, turning once, for medium rare;
10 to 12 minutes for medium to medium-well. Serve with
wedges of lemon.

◆ ◆ ◆ ◆ ◆ **09** ◆ ◆ ◆ ◆ ◆

GARLIC CHICK PEAS
and Greens

2 tablespoons extra-virgin olive oil

6 cloves garlic, crushed

1 pound mustard greens, trimmed and coarsely chopped

Salt and freshly ground black pepper, to taste

1 cup vegetable broth

2 cans (15 ounces each) chick peas, drained

Preheat a skillet over medium heat. Add oil and crushed garlic, sauté 2 minutes, then add greens. Turn and wilt greens in garlic oil and season with salt and pepper. Add vegetable broth to the pan, and bring to a boil. Cover pan, reduce heat and simmer greens, 7 or 8 minutes. Uncover the pan, and stir in chick peas, combining well with the stewed greens. Adjust salt and pepper and serve.

RACHAEL RAY

TOP 30

30-MINUTE MEALS

SIRLOIN BOURGUIGNONNE BURGERS

SERVE *with* GREEN SALAD *and* CHIPS

makes 4 to 6 servings

Sirloin Bourguignonne BURGERS

3/4 to 1 pound ground sirloin

1/4 cup red Burgundy

2 tablespoons fresh thyme, chopped

1 shallot, finely chopped

2 teaspoons Montreal Steak Seasoning blend, or salt
  and freshly ground black pepper, to taste

Extra-virgin olive oil, for drizzling

2 crusty Kaiser rolls, split

1/4 pound (1/2-inch slice) mousse-style pâté

4 cornichon or baby gherkin pickles, thinly sliced
  lengthwise

4 pieces red leaf lettuce

Grainy or Dijon-style mustard

Preheat a grill pan or grill to medium-high heat.

In a large bowl, combine beef with wine, thyme, shallot,
and steak seasoning or salt and pepper. Form meat into
2 large patties, 1 to 1 & 1/2 inches thick. Drizzle patties
with evoo. Cook 5 minutes on each side for medium-
rare, 8 minutes on each side for medium-well.

Toast rolls under hot broiler or in toaster oven. Spread
pâté on bun bottoms. Top with burger, cornichons, and
lettuce. Spread bun tops with mustard and set on burgers. Serve with green salad and chips.

RACHAEL RAY

TOP 30

30-MINUTE MEALS

PECAN-CRUSTED CHICKEN TENDERS

SALAD *with* TANGY MAPLE BARBECUE DRESSING

CHEDDAR & CHIVE BREAD

makes 4 to 6 servings

PECAN-CRUSTED CHICKEN TENDERS *and* Salad with Tangy Maple Barbecue Dressing

Vegetable oil, for frying
1 & 1/3 to 2 pounds chicken tenders
Salt and freshly ground black pepper, to taste
1 cup all-purpose flour
2 eggs, beaten with a splash of milk or water
1 cup plain bread crumbs
1 cup pecans, finely chopped in a food processor
1/2 teaspoon nutmeg, freshly grated or ground
The zest of 1 orange

Dressing:
1/4 cup maple syrup
1/4 cup tangy barbecue sauce
The juice of 1 navel orange
1/4 cup extra-virgin olive oil

Salad:
3 hearts of romaine lettuce, shredded
6 radishes, thinly sliced
6 scallions, trimmed and chopped on an angle
Salt and freshly ground black pepper, to taste

Heat 1 & 1/2 to 2 inches oil over medium-high heat in a skillet.

Season chicken with salt and pepper. Set out 3 shallow dishes. Place flour in one, eggs beaten with water or milk in a second. In the third dish, combine bread crumbs with ground pecans, nutmeg, and orange zest. Coat tenders in batches in flour, then egg, then bread crumbs and pecans. Fry tenders in small batches, 6 to 7 minutes, and drain them on paper towels.

For dressing, combine maple syrup, barbecue sauce and orange juice in a bowl. Whisk in oil, and set aside while cooking the chicken tenders.

Combine romaine, radishes, and scallions in a large salad bowl. Toss with 3/4 of the dressing. Season with salt and pepper, to taste. Top with pecan-crusted chicken tenders and drizzle remaining dressing over top.

"Cooking is more art than science. Your most important instruments are your hands and your palate—learn to trust them.**"**

CHEDDAR & CHIVE BREAD

1 loaf baguette or French bread, split lengthwise, then
  cut in half
2 cups shredded sharp cheddar cheese
10 blades fresh chives, chopped

Heat broiler. Lightly toast bread under hot broiler. Remove
and cover with shredded cheddar cheese. Sprinkle
chopped chives liberally on top and set aside. When
ready to serve your meal, return bread to broiler. When
cheese is bubbly and lightly browned, remove from broiler
and cut into 2-inch slices or large cubes. Use as an alter-
native to croutons, when needed.

RACHAEL RAY

TOP 30

30-MINUTE MEALS

JOHN'S HADDOCK
with BACON, ONIONS AND TOMATOES

WILTED SPINACH
with BUTTER & WINE

makes 2 servings

John's **HADDOCK**

with **Bacon, Onions, and Tomatoes**

1 pound haddock fillet, cut into two portions

1 tablespoon lemon juice

Salt

Extra-virgin olive oil, for drizzling

1/2 tablespoon butter, softened

3 slices smoky bacon, chopped

3 or 4 cippolini, peeled and thinly sliced or a small to
    medium yellow onion, quartered then thinly sliced

1/2 cup Italian bread crumbs

2 to 3 tablespoons chopped fresh flat-leaf parsley

1 plum tomato, seeded and chopped

Preheat the oven to 400°F.

Rinse fish and pat dry. Sprinkle fish with lemon juice and
salt. Coat an oven-safe skillet with a drizzle of evoo and
the softened butter. Set fish into skillet. If your skillet
doesn't have an oven-safe handle, wrap it in tin foil twice
and it should be fine in oven.

Heat a small skillet over medium-high heat. Add a drizzle
of evoo and the bacon. Render the bacon fat 3 minutes,
then add onions. Cook onions until soft, 5 minutes.
Remove pan from heat. Add bread crumbs to the pan
and turn to coat them in drippings. Add parsley and com-

❝When it comes to lighting, candles are an inexpensive cure-all.**❞**

bine. Top fish with coating of bread crumb mixture. Bake 15 minutes. Transfer fish to dinner plates, top with chopped tomato, and serve.

WILTED SPINACH
with Butter & Wine

2 tablespoons butter, cut into small pieces
1 sack (1 pound) triple-washed spinach, tough stems removed and coarsely chopped
1/2 cup dry white wine
Salt and freshly ground black pepper, to taste

Heat a medium skillet over medium heat. Melt butter into pan. Add spinach in bunches, adding more as it wilts down. When all is wilted, add wine and turn to coat. Let wine cook down a minute or two. Season with salt and pepper and serve.

RACHAEL RAY

TOP 30

30-MINUTE MEALS

STEAK
au POIVRE

ARUGULA-STUFFED
TOMATOES

makes 4 servings

STEAK AU POIVRE
and **Arugula-Stuffed Tomatoes**

Tomatoes:

4 vine-ripe tomatoes, red or yellow, tops trimmed and
  seeded

Extra-virgin olive oil, for drizzling

Salt and freshly ground black pepper, to taste

Stuffing:

1/2 cup bread crumbs or 1 slice (1/2-inch thick) stale
  crusty bread, torn

1/2 cup grated Parmigiano Reggiano cheese

1/2 teaspoon crushed red pepper flakes

1 clove garlic, chopped

2 cups arugula leaves

1 tablespoon extra-virgin olive oil

Steaks:

4 New York strip steaks, 1-inch thick

3 tablespoons coarsely ground black pepper

Olive oil to coat skillet

1/4 cup good brandy

2 tablespoons butter

Remove steaks from refrigerator and allow them to come to room temperature for about 10 minutes.

Preheat oven to 400°F.

Arrange tomatoes on broiler pan and drizzle with oil and season with salt and pepper. Combine bread crumbs, cheese, red pepper flakes, garlic, arugula, and 1 table-spoon oil in food processor. Pulse grind to form stuffing. Stuff tomatoes to the rims with mixture and place on center rack of oven. Bake 10 to 12 minutes. Let stand 5 minutes before serving.

Place a heavy-bottomed skillet over medium-high to high heat. Coat steaks liberally on both sides with coarse black pepper. To a very hot pan, drizzle oil to thinly coat the cooking surface. It will smoke. Add steaks immediately. Sear and seal the steaks, cooking them 4 minutes on each side, for medium-rare. For medium to medium-well, reduce heat a bit and cook 5 minutes longer. Remove steaks and let stand 5 minutes. Add brandy to the skillet and warm, then ignite, using a wooden match. Stand back. Let flames burn off, then add butter. Spoon pan juices over steaks. Serve alongside stuffed tomatoes.

RACHAEL RAY

TOP 30

30-MINUTE MEALS

CUBANO BURGERS

MANGO-BLACK BEAN SALSA

SERVE *with* PLANTAIN CHIPS

makes 4 servings

CUBANO BURGERS
with Mango–Black Bean Salsa

Burgers:

1 & 1/3 pounds ground turkey breast

1/3 pound deli-sliced smoked ham, chopped

2 cloves garlic, minced

1/4 red bell pepper, finely chopped

3 scallions, finely chopped

2 tablespoons chopped fresh cilantro

1 tablespoon Montreal Steak Seasoning by McCormick

Vegetable oil or olive oil, for drizzling

8 deli slices (1/3 pound) Swiss cheese

4 Portuguese or crusty Kaiser rolls, split

2 large dill pickles, thinly sliced lengthwise

Sliced banana pepper rings, drained

Yellow mustard

Salsa:

1 jar (16 ounces) black bean salsa

1 ripe mango, peeled and diced

2 tablespoons chopped fresh cilantro

1/4 red bell pepper, finely chopped

"When you eat well, you get to eat more."

Make the burgers: Place turkey in a mixing bowl and add ham, garlic, red bell pepper, scallions, cilantro, and grill seasoning; combine. Form mixture into 4 large patties; drizzle patties with oil.

Heat a large nonstick skillet over medium-high heat. Cook patties until done, 5 to 6 minutes on each side, topping each patty with 2 slices Swiss cheese in the last 2 minutes of cooking time.

Place burgers on bun bottoms and top with sliced dill pickles and banana peppers. Transfer salsa to a serving bowl and top with mango, cilantro, and red bell pepper. Slather the bun tops with mustard and set in place. Serve burgers with plantain chips, and pass salsa for dipping chips or to top burgers.

♦ ♦ ♦ ♦ ♦ **15** ♦ ♦ ♦ ♦ ♦

RACHAEL RAY

TOP
30

30-MINUTE MEALS

GRILLED HALIBUT TACOS
with GUACAMOLE SAUCE

CORN ON THE COB
with CHILI AND LIME

makes 4 servings

GRILLED HALIBUT TACOS
with Guacamole Sauce

4 pieces fresh halibut, steak or fillets (6 to 8 ounces each)

Extra-virgin olive oil, for drizzling

Salt and freshly ground black pepper

The juice of 1 lime

3 small to medium ripe Haas avocados, pitted and
   scooped from skins with a large spoon

The juice of 1 lemon

1/4 teaspoon cayenne pepper

1 cup plain yogurt

1 teaspoon coarse salt

2 plum tomatoes, seeded and chopped

2 scallions, thinly sliced on an angle

1 heart romaine lettuce

12 soft tortillas (6-inch)

Preheat a grill pan or indoor grill to high setting or prepare
outdoor grill. Drizzle halibut on both sides with olive oil.
Season with salt and pepper, to taste. Grill fish, 5 to 6
minutes on each side, or until opaque. Squeeze lime
juice over the fish and remove from the pan or grill. Flake
fish into large chunks with a fork.

While fish is cooking, combine avocado, lemon juice,

cayenne pepper, yogurt, and salt in a blender or food processor. Process until smooth. Remove guacamole to a bowl and stir in tomatoes and scallions. Shred lettuce and reserve.

When fish comes off the grill pan or grill, blister and heat the tortillas. To assemble, pile some of the fish chunks onto tortillas and slather with guacamole sauce. Top with shredded lettuce, fold tacos over and eat!

CORN ON THE COB
with Chili and Lime

4 ears sweet corn, shucked and cleaned
1 lime, cut into wedges
1/3 stick butter, cut into pats
Chili powder, for sprinkling
Salt, to taste

In a medium pot, bring water to a boil and simmer corn, 3 to 5 minutes. Drain and arrange on a plate in a single row. Squeeze lime juice liberally over the ears. Nest pats of butter into paper towels and rub the corn with butter. Season with a sprinkle of chili powder and salt, and serve immediately.

RACHAEL RAY

TOP 30

30-MINUTE MEALS

TUNA STEAK *au* POIVRE

WHITE BEANS *with* ROSEMARY & ROASTED RED PEPPERS

makes 4 servings

TUNA STEAK AU POIVRE
on White Beans with Rosemary & Roasted Red Peppers

4 tuna steaks, 1 & 1/2 inches thick (6 ounces each)

Coarse salt

Extra-virgin olive oil, for drizzling

Coarse freshly ground black pepper

Lemon wedges, for passing

Beans:

2 tablespoons extra-virgin olive oil

2 cloves garlic, finely chopped

1 small onion, chopped

2 cans (15 ounces each) cannellini beans, rinsed and drained

1 roasted red pepper, storebought or homemade, diced (see Note)

2 sprigs fresh rosemary, leaves stripped and finely chopped

A handful chopped fresh flat-leaf parsley

Coarse salt and freshly ground black pepper, to taste

"Beginners allowed! You can make any meal in here, that's my promise."

Preheat a large nonstick skillet or grill pan over high heat. Pat tuna steaks dry and season with a little coarse salt. Drizzle olive oil over tuna to lightly coat on both sides. Season one side of the steaks with a generous coating of coarse ground black pepper. When the pan is very hot, add steaks, peppered-side down. Sear and brown them 2 minutes, then turn and immediately reduce heat to medium. Loosely cover pan with a tin foil tent and allow steaks to cook 2 to 3 minutes for rare, 5 minutes for medium, and 7 minutes for well done.

In a second skillet over moderate heat, coat pan with olive oil, add garlic and onion and sauté, 3 minutes, to soften onion bits. Add beans and chopped roasted red pepper and heat through, 2 to 3 minutes. Stir in rosemary and parsley and season beans with salt and pepper.

Place a serving of beans on a dinner plate and top with Tuna Steak.

Note: To roast red peppers, preheat broiler to high. Halve and seed pepper and place skin-side-up close to hot broiler to blacken skins. Transfer pepper to a brown paper sack and seal to keep in the steam. When cool enough to handle, peel away charred skins.

RACHAEL RAY

TOP 30

30-MINUTE MEALS

URBAN COWBOY
TURKEY BURGERS

SPICY "O-NUTS"

makes 4 servings

Urban Cowboy
TURKEY BURGERS

8 slices turkey or applewood-smoked bacon

1 & 1/3 pounds ground turkey breast

2 cloves garlic, finely chopped

1 large shallot or 1/4 red onion, finely chopped

2 tablespoons chopped fresh thyme or 1 teaspoon dried

2 tablespoons chopped fresh cilantro or parsley

1/2 small green, red, or yellow bell pepper, seeded and finely chopped

1 serrano or jalapeño pepper, seeded and finely chopped

2 teaspoons ground cumin

1 to 2 teaspoons hot sauce, such as Tabasco

2 teaspoons Montreal Steak Seasoning by McCormick

Vegetable oil or olive oil, for drizzling

1/2 pound deli-sliced pepper-Jack cheese

4 crusty Kaiser rolls, split

1 cup sweet red pepper relish or pepper jelly

Red leaf lettuce

Heat a large nonstick skillet over medium-high heat; cook bacon until crisp. Remove bacon, wipe excess grease from skillet, and return skillet to heat.

While bacon is cooking, combine turkey, garlic, shallot or onion, thyme, cilantro or parsley, bell pepper, serrano or jalapeño pepper, cumin, hot sauce, and grill seasoning. Divide mixture into 4 equal mounds then form into patties. Drizzle patties with vegetable oil to coat. Cook in skillet over medium-high heat until done, 5 to 6 minutes on each side, placing sliced cheese over the patties in the last 2 minutes of cooking.

Place cooked cheeseburgers on buns. Spread sweet relish on bun tops and set lettuce into place using relish as "glue." Top cheeseburgers with 2 slices bacon, then serve.

"No fancy equipment or hard-to-find ingredients required."

SPICY "O-NUTS"

Vegetable oil, for frying

1 extra-large sweet onion, peeled, sliced, and
  separated into 3/4-inch-thick rings

2 cups complete pancake mix

1 bottle (12 ounces) cold beer

1 teaspoon sweet paprika

2 teaspoons chili powder

1 tablespoon hot sauce, such as Tabasco

Salt, to taste

Pour 1 inch vegetable oil into a large skillet over medium-high heat. To test the oil, add a 1-inch cube of bread to hot oil; if it turns deep golden brown in a count to 40, the oil is ready.

Place 1/4 cup pancake mix in a resealable bag and add onion rings. Toss to coat onion rings.

Mix together the remaining 1 & 3/4 cups pancake mix, beer, paprika, chili powder, and hot sauce. Working in batches of 5 to 6 slices, coat onion rings in batter and fry until evenly golden brown, 4 to 5 minutes. Transfer to paper towels to drain. Season o-nuts with salt while hot. Repeat with remaining onions. When all the onions are dipped and fried, turn off oil to cool before discarding. Serve o-nuts hot.

RACHAEL RAY

TOP 30

30-MINUTE MEALS

MARINATED GRILLED FLANK STEAK

BLT-SMASHED POTATOES

SERVE *with* STEAMED VEGETABLES

makes 2 servings

Marinated **GRILLED FLANK STEAK** *with* **BLT–Smashed Potatoes**

2 cloves garlic, finely chopped

1 tablespoon Montreal Steak Seasoning by McCormick

1 teaspoon smoked paprika, chili powder, ground
    cumin, or ground chipotles

2 teaspoons hot sauce, such as Tabasco

1 tablespoon Worcestershire sauce

2 tablespoons red wine vinegar (2 splashes)

1/3 cup extra-virgin olive oil, plus a drizzle

1 & 1/2 pounds flank steak

1 & 1/2 pounds small new red-skinned potatoes

1 leek, trimmed of tough tops

4 slices thick-cut smoky bacon, such as applewood-
    smoked, chopped

1 small can (15 ounces) diced tomatoes, well-drained

1/2 cup sour cream, half-and-half, or chicken broth

Salt and freshly ground black pepper, to taste

Mix garlic, grill seasoning, paprika, hot sauce,
Worcestershire sauce, vinegar, and 1/3 cup evoo in a
shallow dish. Place meat in marinade and coat evenly.
Let stand 15 minutes.

Meanwhile, cut larger potatoes in half; leave small ones

"Surprise a few friends with a weeknight invitation— watch a game or just hang out.**"**

whole. Place potatoes in a small pot and cover with water. Cover pot. Bring to a boil, remove lid, then cook until tender, 12 to 15 minutes.

Heat a grill pan or cast-iron pan over high heat.

Cut leek in half lengthwise. Chop into 1/2-inch pieces. Place in a bowl of water and swish, separating the layers, to release the dirt. Drain in a colander or strainer.

Grill flank steak in hot pan; 4 minutes on each side for medium rare to medium, and 6 or 7 minutes for medium-well.

Heat a small skillet over medium-high heat. Add a drizzle of evoo and the bacon. Cook until it begins to crisp and has rendered most of its fat, 3 to 5 minutes. Add leeks and cook until tender, 2 to 3 minutes. Add tomatoes and heat, 1 minute.

Drain potatoes and return them to the hot pot. Smash potatoes with sour cream, half-and-half, or chicken broth and the BLT: bacon, leeks, and tomatoes. Season with salt and pepper.

Remove steak from grill and let it sit a few minutes before slicing. Thinly slice meat on an angle, cutting against the grain. Serve with BLT potatoes and a side of steamed vegetables.

◆ ◆ ◆ ◆ ◆ **19** ◆ ◆ ◆ ◆ ◆

RACHAEL RAY

TOP 30

30-MINUTE MEALS

YOU-WON'T-BE-SINGLE-FOR-LONG VODKA CREAM PASTA

HEART-Y SALAD: HEARTS OF ROMAINE, PALM & ARTICHOKE

makes 2 servings

(with some leftovers)

You-Won't-Be-Single-For-Long
VODKA CREAM PASTA

1 tablespoon extra-virgin olive oil
1 tablespoon butter
2 garlic cloves, minced
2 shallots, minced
1 cup vodka
1 cup chicken stock
1 can (28 ounces) crushed tomatoes
Coarse salt and freshly ground black pepper, to taste
1/2 cup heavy cream
12 ounces pasta, such as penne rigate
20 leaves fresh basil, shredded or torn
Crusty bread

Put large pot of salted water on to boil.

Heat a large skillet over moderate heat. Add oil, butter, garlic, and shallots. Gently sauté garlic and shallots, 3 to 5 minutes. Add vodka, about 3 turns around the pan in a steady stream. Reduce vodka by half, 2 or 3 minutes. Add chicken stock and tomatoes. Bring sauce to a bubble, then reduce heat to simmer. Season with salt and pepper.

While sauce simmers, cook pasta in salted boiling water

until al dente. While pasta cooks, prepare the salad.

Stir cream into vodka sauce. When sauce returns to a bubble, remove from heat. Drain pasta. Toss hot pasta with sauce and basil leaves. Serve immediately, with crusty bread.

HEART-Y SALAD: Hearts of Romaine, Palm & Artichoke

1 heart romaine lettuce, shredded
1 cup fresh flat-leaf parsley leaves (half a bundle)
1 can (14 ounces), hearts of palm, drained
1/4 pound prosciutto di Parma
1 can (15 ounces) quartered artichoke hearts in water, drained
1/4 pound wedge Pecorino, Romano or Asiago cheese
Balsamic vinegar and extra-virgin olive oil, for drizzling
Salt and freshly ground black pepper, to taste

Place romaine on a platter and toss with parsley. Wrap hearts of palm in prosciutto and cut into bite-size pieces on an angle. Arrange palm and artichoke over the romaine. Shave cheese with a vegetable peeler into short ribbons, working over the salad plate. Drizzle with vinegar and oil; season with salt and pepper.

RACHAEL RAY
TOP 30
30-MINUTE MEALS

SWEET 'N SPICY CHICKEN CURRY IN A HURRY WITH FRAGRANT BASMATI RICE

makes 4 servings

Sweet 'n Spicy
CHICKEN CURRY IN A HURRY
with Fragrant Basmati Rice

2 cups basmati rice

1 teaspoon each coriander seeds, cumin seeds, mustard seeds (optional)

2 tablespoons vegetable or canola oil

1 & 1/3 to 1 & 1/2 pounds chicken tenders, diced

2 to 4 cloves garlic, minced (to your taste)

1 to 2 inches fresh gingerroot, minced or grated (to your taste)

1 large yellow onion, chopped

1 can chicken broth (about 2 cups)

2 tablespoons curry paste, mild or hot

1 cup mincemeat (found on the baking aisle)

Coarse salt, to taste

Toppings and garnishes (mix and match):

4 scallions, chopped

1 cup toasted coconut

1/2 cup sliced almonds or Spanish peanuts

1 cup prepared mango chutney

1/4 cup cilantro finely chopped

"Make your own take-out. In as much time as it takes for delivery, you'll have fresh, good-for-you-food.**"**

For spicy rice, toast coriander, cumin, and mustard seeds in the bottom of a medium saucepan. When seeds pop and become fragrant, add water, bring to a boil, and prepare rice according to package directions. For plain rice, prepare as usual.

Heat oil in a large, deep, nonstick skillet over medium-high heat. Add chicken and lightly brown. Add garlic, ginger, and onion, and sauté another 5 minutes. Add chicken broth and bring to a bubble. Stir in curry paste and mincemeat and reduce heat to medium low. Add salt to taste. Simmer, 5 to 10 minutes.

Assemble toppings in small dishes. Serve chicken curry in shallow bowls with scoops of plain or spiced basmati rice. Garnish with your choice of toppings.

RACHAEL RAY

TOP 30

30-MINUTE MEALS

PORTOBELLO BURGERS *with* ROASTED PEPPER SPREAD

SERVE *with* FANCY CHIPS *and* CHUNKED VEGETABLE SALAD

makes 4 "Burgers"

PORTOBELLO BURGERS
with Roasted Pepper Spread

4 medium portobello mushroom caps

Marinade:

3 splashes balsamic vinegar (2 to 3 tablespoons)

3 tablespoons extra-virgin olive oil

4 or 5 dashes Worcestershire sauce

2 sprigs fresh rosemary, leaves stripped from stem, minced

Montreal Steak Seasoning by McCormick or coarse salt
   and black pepper, to taste

4 thin slices provolone cheese, or fresh smoked
   mozzarella

Spread:

1 jar (14 ounces) roasted red pepper, drained, or 3
   homemade roasted peppers

1 clove garlic, cracked from skin

A drizzle extra-virgin olive oil

A handful fresh flat-leaf parsley

A pinch coarse salt and black pepper, to taste

4 pieces Romaine lettuce or arugula

4 thin slices red onion (optional)

4 crusty Kaiser or Italian hard rolls, split and toasted

Quickly rinse and pat dry caps, set aside. Combine marinade, except Montreal Seasoning, in a large plastic food storage bag. Add mushroom caps, seal, and shake to evenly coat.

Heat a nonstick griddle or skillet over medium-high heat. Add portobellos and cook, 3 to 5 minutes on each side, turning once. Season each side with a little steak seasoning or salt and pepper as they cook. Caps should be tender and dark when done. Place a slice of cheese on each cap and remove from heat.

Combine ingredients for the roasted red pepper spread in a food processor and pulse until a paste is formed.

Toast rolls lightly under broiler or toaster oven. Spread generously with roasted pepper. Pile "burgers" in this order: bottom of roll, Portobello with cheese, Romaine or arugula leaves, red onion slice, and roll top. Garnish with fancy chips, such as Yukon Gold onion and garlic chips by Terra brand, and a nice chunked vegetable salad.

RACHAEL RAY

30-MINUTE MEALS

STEAK PIZZAOLA
with **THE WORKS**

ROMAINE SALAD *with*
BLUE CHEESE VINAIGRETTE

makes 2 BIG GUY servings

STEAK PIZZAOLA *with* The Works

1 & 1/2 to 2 pounds porterhouse or rib-eye steak
Salt and freshly ground black pepper
3 tablespoons extra-virgin olive oil
4 cloves garlic, cracked away from the skin
1 teaspoon crushed red pepper flakes
12 mushrooms, sliced
1 small onion, sliced
1 green bell pepper, seeded and sliced
1/3 stick pepperoni, casing removed, chopped (optional)
1/2 cup dry red wine
1 can (28 ounces) crushed tomatoes
1 teaspoon dried oregano or 2 teaspoons chopped fresh
1/4 cup grated Parmigiano Reggiano or Romano cheese

Heat a large nonstick skillet over high heat. Season the steak with salt and pepper. Add 2 tablespoons evoo to the pan, then steak. Brown 3 minutes on each side and remove. Add remaining tablespoon of evoo to pan and reduce heat to medium-high. Add garlic, pepper flakes, mushrooms, onions, bell peppers, and pepperoni, if using. Cook 5 minutes, then add wine and scrape up bits. Add tomatoes, oregano, and salt and pepper to

"Have fun in the kitchen.**"**

taste. Slide steak back in and reduce heat to medium. Cover pan and cook 5 or 6 minutes for medium rare, 10 to 12 minutes for medium well. Remove meat; cut away from bone or divide into 2 large portions. Cover steaks with sauce and top with grated cheese.

ROMAINE SALAD
with **Blue Cheese Vinaigrette**

2 hearts romaine, chopped
1 clove garlic, chopped
1/2 teaspoon dried oregano
2 teaspoons sugar
2 tablespoons red wine vinegar
1/4 cup extra-virgin olive oil
1/4 pound blue cheese crumbles
Salt and freshly ground black pepper, to taste

Place romaine in a big bowl. In a small bowl, combine garlic, oregano, sugar, and vinegar. Add evoo to dressing in a slow stream and mix with a whisk or fork. Stir in blue cheese. Pour dressing over salad and toss. Season with salt and pepper, and serve.

RACHAEL RAY

TOP 30

30-MINUTE MEALS

CAESAR SALAD
THE REAL DEAL, YES, YOU HAVE
TO USE AN EGG,
NO MUSTARD, HOLD THE MAYO

MARK ANTONY'S SCAMPI TOPPING

makes 2 servings

CAESAR SALAD The Real Deal, Yes, You Have to Use an Egg, No Mustard, Hold the Mayo

Croutons:

1 clove garlic

Extra-virgin olive oil

8 to 10 large cubes chewy bread

Salad:

2 large cloves garlic

2 anchovy fillets, plus extra for garnish

1/3 cup extra-virgin olive oil

1 egg yolk (see Note)

4 shakes Worcestershire sauce

1 lemon

3 hearts romaine lettuce

A handful grated Parmigiano Reggiano cheese, plus extra shavings for the table

Cracked black pepper, to taste

Pop a clove of garlic from its skin with a whack using the flat of your knife. Rub the surface of a heavy-bottomed skillet with the cracked clove. Leaving the clove in the skillet, place over medium-low heat and coat the bottom with a thin layer of olive oil. Add the bread. Let it hang out, giving the pan a shake now and then, for 20 minutes, or until cubes are golden brown.

Rub the sides and bottom of your salad bowl, all the better if it's wooden, with the two garlic cloves you'll use in the dressing. After rubbing the bowl, place the garlic pieces, anchovies, and olive oil in a small saucepan. Heat over medium heat until anchovies melt completely into the oil; their fishy flavor will not be distinguishable— just a nice, subtle, salty but almost nutty presence will remain. Remove the garlic and discard. (The oil will be infused with the flavor.) Pour the oil into the bottom of the salad bowl. Separate the egg. Discard the white. Mix yolk into oil with a fork. Add Worcestershire. Roll lemon on counter to release juices. Cut lemon in half and squeeze juice into bowl. Mix vigorously with fork. Coarsely chop the lettuce hearts and dump into bowl. Add cheese, a lot of pepper, and croutons. Coat the salad completely, tossing and turning several times. Serve with extra cheese and pepper.

Note: If you're worried about the raw egg, use a splash of pasteurized egg product.

"When a special occasion comes up, why not choose to stay in—in style!"

Mark Antony's
SCAMPI TOPPING

2 cloves garlic, minced
A pinch crushed red pepper flakes
2 tablespoons extra-virgin olive oil
10 jumbo shrimp, peeled and deveined
A shot white wine

Heat garlic and crushed red pepper in oil over medium-high heat until the garlic speaks. Add shrimp and cook for a minute on each side, keeping pan moving with vigorous shakes to avoid burning garlic. Douse with a little white wine and serve on top of Caesar greens.

RACHAEL RAY

TOP 30

30-MINUTE MEALS

CHICKEN PICCATA PASTA TOSS

EMMANUEL'S BAKED ARTICHOKE HEARTS

makes 4 servings

Emmanuel's Baked
ARTICHOKE HEARTS

2 cans (15 ounces each) artichoke hearts in water, 6 to
   8 count, drained
1 tablespoon extra-virgin olive oil, plus a drizzle for
   baking dish
The juice of 1/4 lemon
1 tablespoon butter
3 cloves garlic, chopped
6 anchovy fillets
1 cup Italian-style bread crumbs (3 handfuls)
1/4 cup chopped fresh flat-leaf parsley
1/4 cup grated Parmigiano Reggiano
Coarse freshly ground black pepper

Preheat oven to 400°F.

Turn artichokes upside down to get all the liquid out, and
cut them in half lengthwise. Drizzle a small casserole dish
with a little olive oil, spreading it with a pastry brush.
Arrange artichokes with tops up, bottoms down, in a lay-
ered pattern in the dish. Top with lemon juice.

Preheat a small nonstick skillet over medium heat. Add oil
and butter to the skillet. When the butter melts into the
oil, add garlic and anchovies. Using the back of a wood-
en spoon, work the anchovies into the oil as they break

up. When anchovies have dissolved, add bread crumbs and lightly toast, about 2 to 3 minutes. Add parsley, cheese, and pepper, stir to combine and remove from heat. Top artichokes with an even layer of bread topping and set in the middle of oven. Bake until topping is deep golden brown, about 10 minutes.

CHICKEN PICCATA Pasta Toss

1 pound penne rigate pasta, cooked al dente

2 tablespoons extra-virgin olive oil

1 & 1/4 pounds chicken tenders, cut into 1-inch pieces

Salt and freshly ground black pepper, to taste

2 tablespoons butter

4 cloves garlic, chopped

2 medium shallots, chopped

2 tablespoons flour

1/2 cup white wine

The juice of 1 lemon

1 cup chicken broth or stock

3 tablespoons capers, drained

1/2 cup chopped fresh flat-leaf parsley

Chopped or snipped chives, for garnish

Heat a deep nonstick skillet over medium-high heat. Add 1 tablespoon of olive oil and the chicken to the pan. Season with salt and pepper, and brown until lightly golden, about 5 to 6 minutes. Remove chicken from pan and set it in your serving dish while you complete the sauce.

Return the skillet to the heat, reduced to medium. To the skillet, add another tablespoon olive oil, 1 tablespoon butter, the garlic and the shallots and sauté, 3 minutes. Stir in flour and cook, 2 minutes. Whisk in wine and reduce liquid, 1 minute. Whisk lemon juice and broth into sauce. Stir in capers and parsley. When sauce comes to a bubble, add remaining tablespoon butter to give it a little shine.

Put chicken back in the pan and heat through a minute or two. Toss hot pasta with chicken and sauce. Adjust salt and pepper to taste. Top with fresh snipped chives and serve.

RACHAEL RAY

TOP 30

30-MINUTE MEALS

BARBECUE SAUCY SALMON

ROMAINE SALAD *with* ORANGE VINAIGRETTE

makes 2 servings

Barbecue Saucy SALMON *on* Romaine Salad with Orange Vinaigrette

Salmon and Barbecue Glaze:

1 tablespoon extra-virgin olive oil, plus a little for drizzling

1/4 red onion, finely chopped

2 tablespoons red wine vinegar

1/2 cup maple syrup

1 tablespoon tomato paste

2 teaspoons Worcestershire sauce

1 teaspoon curry powder

2 to 3 drops Liquid Smoke

1/2 teaspoon freshly ground black pepper

2 salmon fillets or salmon steaks (6 to 8 ounces each)

Salt

Salad and Dressing:

The zest and juice of 1 small navel orange

1 clove garlic, finely chopped

2 teaspoons Dijon mustard

2 tablespoons chopped fresh tarragon or 1 teaspoon dried

1 teaspoon salt

1/4 cup extra-virgin olive oil

2 hearts romaine lettuce

3 scallions, chopped

Make the glaze: Heat a small saucepan over medium heat, add evoo then onion, and cook onion 3 minutes. Add vinegar and cook until reduced by half. Add syrup, tomato paste, Worcestershire, curry, Liquid Smoke, and pepper. Bring to a bubble and simmer.

Meanwhile, start the salmon: Heat a grill pan over medium-high heat. Drizzle salmon with evoo and season with salt. Grill for 3 minutes and baste liberally with the glaze. Flip salmon and glaze opposite side. If you like your salmon pink at the center, remove after another 3 minutes; for opaque salmon, grill 5 minutes on each side.

Make the salad: Whisk orange zest and juice with garlic, Dijon, tarragon, and salt, then stream in evoo, whisking to combine. Chop lettuce and toss with scallions and dressing. Pile salad onto plates and top with glazed barbecued salmon.

RACHAEL RAY

TOP 30

30-MINUTE MEALS

DELMONICO STEAKS *with* BALSAMIC ONIONS *and* STEAK SAUCE

BLUE CHEESE & WALNUT SPINACH SALAD *with* MAPLE DRESSING

makes 4 servings

DELMONICO STEAKS
with Balsamic Onions and Steak Sauce

4 Delmonico steaks, 1-inch thick (10 to 12 ounces each)

2 teaspoons extra-virgin olive oil

Montreal Steak Seasoning by McCormick or coarse salt and black pepper, to taste

Onions:

1 tablespoon extra-virgin olive oil

2 large yellow onions, thinly sliced

1/4 cup balsamic vinegar

Steak Sauce:

1 & 1/2 teaspoons extra-virgin olive oil

2 cloves garlic, chopped

1 small white boiling onion, chopped

1/4 cup dry cooking sherry

1 cup canned tomato sauce

1 tablespoon Worcestershire sauce

Freshly ground black pepper, to taste

Heat a heavy grill pan or griddle pan over high heat, and wipe it with olive oil using tongs and a paper towel. Cook steaks 4 minutes on each side for medium, 7 to 8 minutes for medium well. Season with steak seasoning or salt and pepper and remove to a warm platter.

Onions: Heat a medium nonstick skillet over medium-high heat. Add oil and sliced yellow onions and cook, stirring occasionally, 10 to 12 minutes, until onions are soft and sweet. Add balsamic vinegar to the pan and turn onions until vinegar cooks away and glazes onions a deep brown, 3 to 5 minutes.

Steak Sauce: Heat a small saucepan over medium heat. Add oil, garlic and white onions and sauté, 5 minutes until tender. Add sherry to the pan and combine with onions. Stir in tomato sauce and Worcestershire and season with black pepper.

To serve, top steaks with onions and drizzle a little steak sauce down over the top, reserving half to pass at table.

Blue Cheese & Walnut SPINACH SALAD *with* Maple Dressing

1 sack (10 ounces) baby spinach
1/3 pound blue cheese, crumbled
1 can (6 ounces) walnut halves, toasted
1/4 cup maple syrup, warmed
1 & 1/2 tablespoons cider vinegar
1/4 cup extra-virgin olive oil
Salt and freshly ground black pepper

Place spinach on a large platter. Top with blue cheese and walnuts. Warm maple syrup in a small saucepan. Pour vinegar into a small bowl. Whisk oil into vinegar in a slow stream, then whisk in maple syrup slowly. Pour dressing over the salad and serve. Season with salt and pepper, to taste.

RACHAEL RAY

TOP 30

30-MINUTE MEALS

SAGE VEAL CHOPS

ARUGULA SALAD
with **BLUE CHEESE, PEARS,**
AND APRICOT VINAIGRETTE

makes 4 servings

SAGE VEAL CHOPS

4 veal chops, 1-inch thick

Salt and freshly ground black pepper, to taste

6 sprigs fresh sage, chopped (about 4 tablespoons)

1 tablespoon extra-virgin olive oil

2 tablespoons butter

1/2 cup dry white wine

Heat a heavy-bottomed skillet over medium-high heat. Season chops with salt and pepper and rub them each with about 1 tablespoon of chopped sage, rubbing well into both sides of the chops. Add oil to the pan. Melt butter into the oil and add chops to the pan. Cook 5 minutes on each side, remove to warm platter, and let rest. Add wine to the pan and scrape up the drippings. Spoon over the chops and serve.

ARUGULA SALAD *with* Blue Cheese, Pears, and Apricot Vinaigrette

2 bunches arugula, washed and dried, stems trimmed
1 head Bibb lettuce, torn
The juice of 1/2 lemon
1 ripe pear, thinly sliced
1/2 pound Maytag or other blue cheese, crumbled

Dressing:

1 small shallot, minced
2 tablespoons white wine vinegar
1/4 cup apricot all-fruit spread
1/3 cup extra-virgin olive oil
Salt and freshly ground black pepper, to taste

Combine arugula and lettuce in a salad bowl. Squeeze a little lemon juice over pear slices to keep them from browning. Arrange them on top of the lettuce and arugula. Top with blue cheese crumbles.

To make the dressing, combine shallots, vinegar, and apricot spread in a bowl. Stream in oil as you whisk. Add to salad, season with salt and black pepper and serve.

RACHAEL RAY

TOP 30

30-MINUTE MEALS

TUNA BURGERS
with **GINGER AND SOY**

GRILLED RED ONIONS

SERVE *with*
ROOT VEGETABLE CHIPS
and **PICKLED GINGER**

makes 4 servings

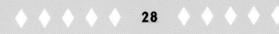

GUY*food*

TUNA BURGERS
with Ginger and Soy

1 & 1/2 pounds fresh tuna steak

2 cloves garlic, chopped

2 inches fresh gingerroot, minced or grated

3 tablespoons Tamari (dark soy sauce)

2 scallions, chopped

1/2 small red bell pepper, finely chopped

2 teaspoons sesame oil

2 teaspoons Montreal Steak Seasoning by McCormick,
   or 1 teaspoon freshly ground black pepper, and 1/2
   teaspoon of salt

1 tablespoon light-colored oil, such as canola or
   vegetable

1/2 pound shiitake mushrooms, coarsely chopped

Coarse salt, to taste

4 sesame Kaiser rolls

1 jar (8 ounces) mango chutney

4 leaves red leaf lettuce

1 jar (8 ounces) wasabi or Asian sweet hot mustard

Pickled ginger, for garnish (optional)

Preheat a nonstick griddle or a grill pan to medium-high to high heat. Cube tuna into bite-size pieces and place in a food processor. Pulse the processor to grind the tuna until it has the consistency of ground beef. Transfer to a bowl. Combine ground tuna with garlic, ginger, soy sauce, scallions, red bell pepper, sesame oil, and Montreal Seasoning or salt and black pepper. Form 4 large patties, 1 & 1/2 inches thick. Drizzle patties on both sides with oil.

Cook tuna burgers 2 to 3 minutes on each side for rare, up to 6 minutes each side for well done.

In a medium nonstick skillet over medium-high heat, sauté fresh shiitakes for 2 or 3 minutes in 1 tablespoon oil (once around the pan in a slow stream). Season mushrooms with salt and pepper.

Split the rolls and lightly toast them under broiler. Spread mango chutney on the bottom of each bun. Top with tuna burger, shiitakes, and lettuce. Spread wasabi mustard or sweet hot mustard on bun tops and set them in place. Serve with root vegetable chips and pickled ginger, if desired.

Grilled **RED ONIONS**

1 large red onion, unpeeled

Light-colored oil such as canola or vegetable, for
  drizzling

Montreal Steak Seasoning by McCormick, or coarse
  salt and freshly ground black pepper, to taste

Preheat a grill or nonstick griddle to hot. Trim a thin slice
off the side of the unpeeled onion. Set the onion flat on
the cut surface for stability. Cut the onion into 4 one-inch-
thick slices. Remove the outer ring of skin from each
slice. Drizzle the sliced onion with light-colored oil and
season both sides with steak seasoning or salt and pepper. Grill on hot grill or on a nonstick griddle for 5 to 7
minutes on each side, until onion is tender and has
begun to caramelize. Serve alongside tuna burgers.

RACHAEL RAY

TOP 30

30-MINUTE MEALS

MUSSELS *in* MEXICAN BEER

CHORIZO & SHRIMP
QUESADILLAS *with*
SMOKY GUACAMOLE

makes 2 servings

MUSSELS *in* Mexican beer

2 tablespoons extra-virgin olive oil

4 cloves garlic, cracked away from skin and crushed

1 small onion, chopped

1 jalapeño, seeded and chopped

A couple pinches salt

2 dozen mussels, scrubbed

1/2 cup dark Mexican beer, such as Negro Modelo

1 can (15 ounces), diced tomatoes, drained

2 tablespoons chopped fresh flat-leaf parsley or
  cilantro

In a deep skillet with a cover, preheated over medium-high heat, add evoo, garlic, onion, and jalapeño. Season with salt. Sauté 2 minutes. Arrange mussels in the pan. Pour in beer and tomatoes and shake the pan to combine. Cover and cook 3 to 5 minutes or until mussels open. Remove from heat and spoon sauce down into shells. Garnish with parsley or cilantro. Serve immediately from the pan.

CHORIZO & SHRIMP QUESADILLAS
with Smoky Guacamole

Guacamole:

2 ripe Haas avocados

The juice of 1 lime

A couple pinches salt

1/4 cup sour cream (3 rounded tablespoons)

2 chipotle peppers in adobo (available in cans in
   Mexican section of market)

Quesadillas:

1/2 pound chorizo sausage, sliced thin on an angle

1 tablespoon extra-virgin olive oil, plus some for drizzling

1 clove garlic, cracked away from skin and crushed

12 large shrimp, peeled and deveined, tails removed
   (ask for easy-peels at seafood counter)

Salt and freshly ground black pepper, to taste

4 twelve-inch flour tortillas

1/2 pound (2 cups) shredded pepper-Jack cheese

"The kitchen table is where it's at."

HOW TO MEASURE RACHAEL'S WAY:

A HANDFUL
about 3 tablespoons

◆

A PALMFUL
about 2 tablespoons

◆

HALF A PALMFUL
you do the math

◆

A PINCH
about 1/4 teaspoon

◆

A FEW GOOD PINCHES
about 1 teaspoon

◆

ONCE AROUND THE PAN
about 1 tablespoon of liquid

◆

TWICE AROUND THE PAN
more math: about 2 tablespoons,
3 or 4 would be 1/4 cup

◆

RACHAEL RAY

TOP 30

30-MINUTE MEALS

OUTSIDE-IN
BACON CHEESEBURGERS *with*
GREEN ONION MAYO

BEEFSTEAK TOMATO &
VIDALIA ONION SALAD
with STEAK SAUCE DRESSING

makes 6 servings

Outside-In
BACON CHEESEBURGERS
with Green Onion Mayo

6 slices bacon, chopped

4 scallions, cleaned and trimmed

Extra-virgin olive oil, for drizzling

1 & 3/4 pounds ground beef sirloin

1 & 1/2 tablespoons Worcestershire sauce

1 & 1/2 tablespoons Montreal Steak Seasoning by McCormick, or coarse salt and fresh black pepper

3/4 pound extra-sharp white cheddar cheese, crumbled

1 cup mayonnaise or reduced-fat mayonnaise

1 teaspoon ground cumin

Salt and freshly ground black pepper

6 crusty Kaiser rolls, split

6 leaves crisp romaine lettuce

Preheat grill pan over high heat.

In a medium pan, brown bacon and drain on a paper towel–lined plate.

Brush scallions with a little evoo and grill on hot grill pan 2 or 3 minutes on each side. Remove from heat to cool.

Combine ground beef with Worcestershire and steak seasoning or salt and pepper. Divide meat into 6 equal parts. Combine cheese crumbles and cooked bacon. Take a portion of the ground meat in your hand and make a well in the center. Pile in cheese and bacon, then carefully form the burger around the filling. Make sure the fillings are completely covered with meat. When all 6 patties are formed, drizzle burgers with evoo and place on hot grill pan. Cook 2 minutes on each side over high heat, reduce heat to medium-low and cook burgers 7 or 8 minutes longer, turning occasionally. Do not press down on burgers as they cook. Transfer to a plate and let them rest 5 minutes before serving.

Make the mayonnaise: Chop cooled, grilled green onions and add to a food processor. Add mayonnaise and cumin and pulse-grind together. Season with salt and pepper to taste.

Place burgers on crusty buns and top with crisp lettuce leaves and a slather of green onion mayonnaise.

“Heads up: read through a recipe before you start cooking.**”**

BEEFSTEAK TOMATO & VIDALIA ONION SALAD *with*
Steak Sauce Dressing

1/4 cup red wine vinegar

3 rounded tablespoons brown sugar

1 tablespoon Worcestershire sauce

1 teaspoon coarse black pepper

1 cup canned tomato sauce

2 tablespoons extra-virgin olive oil

4 beefsteak tomatoes, sliced 1/2-inch thick

1 large Vidalia onion, peeled and cut into 1/2-inch thick rings

Salt, to taste

3 tablespoons chopped parsley, for garnish

Make the dressing: In a small saucepan over moderate heat combine vinegar, sugar, Worcestershire, and pepper. Allow sugar to dissolve and liquids to come to a bubble. Remove sauce from heat and whisk in tomato sauce, then evoo. Serve warm or chilled.

Arrange sliced tomatoes and onions on a serving platter. Season with salt. Pour dressing over the tomatoes and onions and garnish with chopped parsley.

RACHAEL RAY

TOP 30

30-MINUTE MEALS

MANLY MANNY'S CHILI

SERVE *with* CORN CHIPS

makes 6 servings

Manly Manny's CHILI

2 tablespoons corn or vegetable oil

1 large onion, chopped fine

4 cloves garlic, minced

1 & 1/2 pounds ground sirloin, 90% lean

Montreal Steak Seasoning or salt and pepper, to taste

1/2 bottle beer (6 ounces)

1 can (14 ounces) beef broth

1 can (6 ounces) tomato paste

1 & 1/2 tablespoons dark chili powder

1 tablespoon ground cumin

2 ounces smoky barbecue sauce (2 glugs)

2 ounces hot sauce (about 3 tablespoons)

6 ounces shredded smoked cheddar cheese

Chopped raw onions (optional)

Heat oil in a deep pot over medium-high heat. Add onions and garlic; sauté 3 to 5 minutes, stirring frequently. Add beef and brown, another 3 to 5 minutes. Season lightly with Montreal seasoning or salt and pepper. Add beer and let it reduce by half.

Stir in broth, paste, chili powder, cumin, barbecue sauce, and hot sauce. Reduce heat to medium low and simmer 10 minutes. Top with cheddar and onions, if using. Serve with corn chips.

RACHAEL RAY

TOP
30

30-MINUTE MEALS

BLACKENED CHICKEN PIZZA *with* YELLOW TOMATO SALSA

SERVE *with* GREEN SALAD

makes 2 servings

BLACKENED CHICKEN PIZZA
with Yellow Tomato Salsa

1 tablespoon Montreal Steak Seasoning by McCormick

1 teaspoon sweet paprika

1 teaspoon chili powder

1/2 teaspoon cayenne pepper or a few drops hot sauce

1/2 to 3/4 pound chicken breast, sliced thin

1 tablespoon vegetable oil

All-purpose flour or corn meal, for dusting

1 store-bought pizza dough

1/2 pound brick reduced-fat cheese with jalapeño
  pepper, such as Cabot brand

2 small yellow tomatoes, seeded and chopped

1/4 cup chopped red onion

1 jalapeño pepper, seeded and finely chopped

2 tablespoons cilantro (optional)

2 tablespoons fresh thyme leaves

1 clove garlic, cracked away from skins

Salt, to taste

The zest and juice of 1/2 lime

Preheat oven to 450°F.

Heat a large, heavy skillet over very high heat. Combine grill seasoning, paprika, chili powder, and cayenne pepper on a plate. Press chicken slices into seasoning on one side. Add oil to screaming hot pan and cook chicken 2 minutes on each side. Remove chicken from skillet and chop.

Sprinkle a little flour or corn meal on a pizza pan or cookie sheet and stretch out pizza dough on pan. Shred reduced-fat cheese.

Make the salsa: Combine tomatoes, onion, jalapeño, cilantro (if using), and thyme. Make a garlic paste by chopping garlic then adding a generous pinch of salt and mashing it together with the flat of the knife. Add garlic paste to salsa. Add lime zest and juice and mix salsa well.

Scatter chicken, salsa, and cheese over pizza dough, working to the edges. Bake until crisp and bubbly-brown on top, 12 to 15 minutes. Serve with a green salad, dressed in lime juice, olive oil, salt, and pepper.

RACHAEL RAY

TOP 30

30-MINUTE MEALS

GRILLED MAHI-MAHI FILLETS

ASPARAGUS *with* ORANGE AND SESAME

makes 4 servings

Grilled **MAHI-MAHI** Fillets

4 portions mahi-mahi fillets (6 to 8 ounces each)
Salt and freshly ground black pepper, to taste
The juice of 2 limes
3 tablespoons Tamari dark soy sauce
2 inches fresh gingerroot, grated (1 & 1/2 tablespoons)
1 tablespoon vegetable or canola oil
20 blades fresh chives, chopped or 3 scallions, thinly
   sliced, for garnish

Preheat grill pan over medium-high to high heat. Season
mahi-mahi fillets with salt and pepper. Combine lime
juice, dark soy, ginger, and a little vegetable or canola oil
in a shallow dish. Turn fish in the citrus-soy marinade and
let it "hang out" for 10 minutes. Grill 4 to 5 minutes per
side or until fish is firm and opaque.

"Relax! You're not racing the clock, you're only making dinner.**"**

ASPARAGUS
with Orange and Sesame

2 navel oranges
1 inch fresh gingerroot, peeled
Salt
1 to 1 & 3/4 pounds thin asparagus spears, trimmed
2 tablespoons toasted sesame seeds

Cut the ends off two navel oranges and stand them upright on a cutting board. Remove skins in strips using a sharp knife to cut down from the top of the orange. Reserve the peels of 1 orange. When peeled and trimmed, slice into 1/4-inch rounds, and set aside.

In a skillet with cover, bring 1-inch of water to a boil with the peels of 1 orange and the gingerroot. When the water boils, add a healthy pinch of salt and asparagus spears. Simmer 3 to 5 minutes until just tender, then drain. Assemble a few spears on each dinner plate, crisscrossing the spears and orange slices. Finish with a sprinkle of sesame seeds and top with 1 portion of grilled mahi mahi. Garnish plates with chopped chives and serve.

RACHAEL RAY

TOP 30

30-MINUTE MEALS

TRIPLE-A PASTA: SPINACH PASTA *with* ASPARAGUS, ARTICHOKE, AND ARUGULA

SERVE *with* CRUSTY BREAD *and* FRESH SLICED MELON

Serves 4

TRIPLE-A PASTA:
Spinach Pasta *with* Asparagus, Artichoke, and Arugula

12 ounces spinach fettuccine, dried or fresh, cooked
  until al dente

Extra-virgin olive oil, a drizzle

1 tablespoon butter

2 tablespoons extra-virgin olive oil

1 large or 2 medium shallots, finely chopped

1/2 cup white wine

1 pound thin fresh asparagus spears, trimmed and cut
  on angle into bite-size pieces

1 cup broth, chicken or vegetable

1 can (14 ounces) artichoke hearts in water, drained
  and chopped

24 leaves fresh arugula, torn or coarsely chopped

2 tablespoons zest from 1 large lemon (grate skin, not
  the white part)

Coarse salt and black pepper, to taste

A handful chopped fresh flat-leaf parsley, to garnish

Drain pasta well and drizzle with oil to keep from sticking. Set aside.

Heat a large, deep skillet over medium heat. Add butter and olive oil to pan and heat until butter is melted. Add shallots and sauté, 3 minutes. Add wine and reduce liquid by half, about 2 minutes more. Add asparagus bits, cover, and cook, 3 or 4 minutes. Then uncover, adding broth and artichokes to pan. Heat artichokes through and add cooked pasta. Sprinkle in arugula. Toss ingredients until arugula wilts. Season with lemon zest, salt and pepper, and parsley, to taste.

Serve immediately with crusty bread. Fresh sliced melon makes a simple and wonderful accompaniment to this meal.

RACHAEL RAY

TOP 30

30-MINUTE MEALS

VEAL SCALOPPINI
with WINE, MUSHROOMS, AND GREEN OLIVES

SERVE *with* GREEN SALAD

makes 4 servings

VEAL SCALOPPINI *with* Wine, Mushrooms, and Green Olives

3/4 pound linguini

Salt and freshly ground black pepper, to taste

1/4 cup extra-virgin olive oil, plus some for drizzling

3 slices pancetta or bacon, chopped

1 small onion, chopped

16 crimini or button mushrooms, chopped

1 pound veal scaloppini, cut into 1-inch strips

2 cloves garlic, smashed

1 cup dry white wine

16 pitted, large green olives, coarsely chopped

A handful chopped, fresh flat-leaf Italian parsley

1 tablespoon butter, cut into pieces

1/3 cup grated Parmigiano Reggiano or Romano cheese (a couple handfuls)

"If you keep those pots rocking, your date will keep on knocking…at your door.**"**

In a big pot, bring water to boil, add salt, and cook linguini 8 minutes, to al dente.

Preheat a large heavy skillet over medium to medium-high heat. Add 1 tablespoon olive oil and the pancetta or bacon. Cook 1 to 2 minutes, then add onions and cook, another 2 to 3 minutes. Add mushrooms and cook, another 3 to 5 minutes.

While vegetables are cooking, season veal strips with salt and pepper. To a second skillet preheated over medium-high heat, add 1 & 1/2 tablespoons olive oil and 1 clove smashed garlic. Quick-fry half of the veal, searing each side of the strips, 1 to 2 minutes. Transfer to a plate and repeat with remaining veal. When done, add all of the veal and garlic to the onions and mushrooms, then add wine to the veal pan and scrape up the drippings. Cook wine down (and alcohol out), 2 to 3 minutes. Stir olives and parsley into veal and mushrooms, and serve on a bed of hot linguini tossed with a drizzle of olive oil, butter, and grated cheese. Serve with a green salad on the side.

RACHAEL RAY

TOP 30

30-MINUTE MEALS

TENDERLOIN STEAKS *with* GORGONZOLA

ROAST POTATOES *with* ROSEMARY

makes 4 servings

TENDERLOIN STEAKS
with Gorgonzola

4 beef tenderloin steaks, 1 & 1/2-inches thick, at room
  temperature

1 tablespoon extra-virgin olive oil

Salt and freshly ground black pepper, to taste

3/4 pound gorgonzola cheese

4 leaves fresh sage, thinly sliced

Place a large, flat griddle or skillet over high heat. When it
is hot, wipe the surface with oil using a pair of tongs and
a folded paper towel. Place steaks on hot pan and
caramelize, 2 minutes on each side. Reduce heat to
moderate and cook 4 to 5 minutes longer. Season with
salt and pepper.

Preheat broiler to high.

Arrange steaks on a baking sheet and top each with 3
ounces cheese. Place sheet 6 inches from broiler and
heat just long enough to melt the cheese. Remove from
the oven and top with sage. Let meat rest up to 5 minutes, allowing the juices to redistribute. Serve with roast
potatoes and a green salad.

ROAST POTATOES *with*
Rosemary

2 pounds small potatoes, baby Yukon gold or red skin

6 cloves garlic, cracked away from skin

2 to 3 tablespoons extra-virgin olive oil (just enough to coat potatoes)

2 tablespoons fresh rosemary leaves, chopped

Salt and freshly ground black pepper, to taste

Preheat oven to 500°F or highest setting.

Halve potatoes and place on a cookie sheet. Combine with garlic. Coat potatoes and garlic with oil and season with rosemary, salt, and pepper.

Place on lower rack of oven and roast 20 to 25 minutes, turning potatoes once after about 12 minutes. Continue roasting until golden and crisp at edges.

RACHAEL RAY

TOP 30

30-MINUTE MEALS

CRISPY CHICKEN CUTLETS
with BASIL-PARSLEY SAUCE

CHEESY RISI E BISI

makes 4 servings

CHEESY RISI E BISI

2 tablespoons extra-virgin olive oil
1 large clove garlic, finely chopped
1 small onion, finely chopped
1 cup Arborio rice
Salt and freshly ground black pepper, to taste
1/2 cup dry white wine
3 to 4 cups chicken broth
1/4 to 1/3 cup grated Parmigiano Reggiano cheese
2 tablespoons chopped fresh flat-leaf parsley
1 cup tiny frozen peas, thawed

Heat a medium skillet over medium-high heat. Add evoo, then garlic and onion and sauté, stirring constantly, 2 to 3 minutes. Add rice and a little salt and pepper. Cook another minute, then add wine and cook until wine is completely absorbed, 30 seconds. Add about 1 cup chicken broth and stir. Reduce heat to medium and cook until broth is absorbed, stirring often. Continue adding 1/2 cup broth each time liquid is completely absorbed, stirring all the while. Use as much broth as is needed to result in creamy, slightly chewy rice; takes about 22 minutes. Work on chicken while rice continues to cook; recipe follows.

When rice is cooked to desired consistency, remove from heat and stir in cheese, parsley, and peas.

CRISPY CHICKEN CUTLETS
with **Basil-Parsley Sauce**

2 pounds chicken cutlets

Salt and freshly ground black pepper

3 to 4 tablespoons all-purpose flour

1 cup Italian bread crumbs

1/3 to 1/2 cup grated Parmigiano Reggiano cheese

1 teaspoon crushed red pepper flakes

2 teaspoons poultry seasoning (half a palmful)

1 clove garlic

1 jar (3 ounces) pine nuts (pignoli)

The zest of 1 lemon (2 tablespoons)

2 eggs, beaten

Olive oil, for frying

1 plum tomato, seeded and finely chopped, for garnish

Sauce:

1 cup loosely packed basil leaves

1/2 cup loosely packed fresh flat-leaf parsley leaves

The juice of 1/2 lemon

Salt and freshly ground black pepper, to taste

1/4 cup extra-virgin olive oil

Season cutlets with salt and pepper on both sides. Place flour in a shallow dish and turn cutlets lightly in flour.

Combine bread crumbs, cheese, red pepper flakes, poultry seasoning, garlic, pine nuts, and lemon zest in a food processor and pulse-process to evenly mix. Transfer the mixture to a plate. Beat eggs in a separate shallow dish.

Heat a thin layer of oil, just enough to coat the bottom of the pan, in a large skillet over medium to medium-high heat. Coat cutlets in eggs then breading and place in hot oil. Cook cutlets in a single layer, in 2 batches if necessary, until breading is evenly browned and juices run clear, 3 or 4 minutes on each side. Remove to a plate and tent with aluminum foil to keep warm.

Make the sauce: Return food processor bowl to base and add basil, parsley, and lemon juice. Add a little salt and pepper. Turn processor on and stream in evoo until a loose paste forms.

Serve chicken cutlets with a generous topping of basil and parsley sauce. Garnish with tomato.

RACHAEL RAY

TOP 30

30-MINUTE MEALS

MOROCCAN RUB LAMB CHOPS

GARLIC CHICK PEAS *and* GREENS

makes 4 servings

Moroccan Rub LAMB CHOPS

12 loin lamb chops
1 tablespoon extra-virgin olive oil
1 tablespoon ground cumin
2 teaspoons ground turmeric
1 teaspoon sweet paprika
1 teaspoon coriander seeds
1 teaspoon garlic salt
1/2 teaspoon hot red pepper flakes
1 lemon, wedged

Preheat grill pan to high. Brush chops with a little olive oil.
Mix dry spices in a small container, cover and shake to
combine. Rub spice blend into the chops on both sides,
and grill 7 to 8 minutes, turning once, for medium rare;
10 to 12 minutes for medium to medium-well. Serve with
wedges of lemon.

GARLIC CHICK PEAS
and Greens

2 tablespoons extra-virgin olive oil

6 cloves garlic, crushed

1 pound mustard greens, trimmed and coarsely
   chopped

Salt and freshly ground black pepper, to taste

1 cup vegetable broth

2 cans (15 ounces each) chick peas, drained

Preheat a skillet over medium heat. Add oil and crushed
garlic, sauté 2 minutes, then add greens. Turn and wilt
greens in garlic oil and season with salt and pepper. Add
vegetable broth to the pan, and bring to a boil. Cover
pan, reduce heat and simmer greens, 7 or 8 minutes.
Uncover the pan, and stir in chick peas, combining well
with the stewed greens. Adjust salt and pepper and
serve.

♦ ♦ ♦ ♦ ♦ **10** ♦ ♦ ♦ ♦ ♦

RACHAEL RAY

TOP 30

30-MINUTE MEALS

SIRLOIN BOURGUIGNONNE BURGERS

SERVE *with* GREEN SALAD *and* CHIPS

makes 4 to 6 servings

48

Sirloin Bourguignonne BURGERS

3/4 to 1 pound ground sirloin

1/4 cup red Burgundy

2 tablespoons fresh thyme, chopped

1 shallot, finely chopped

2 teaspoons Montreal Steak Seasoning blend, or salt and freshly ground black pepper, to taste

Extra-virgin olive oil, for drizzling

2 crusty Kaiser rolls, split

1/4 pound (1/2-inch slice) mousse-style pâté

4 cornichon or baby gherkin pickles, thinly sliced lengthwise

4 pieces red leaf lettuce

Grainy or Dijon-style mustard

Preheat a grill pan or grill to medium-high heat.

In a large bowl, combine beef with wine, thyme, shallot, and steak seasoning or salt and pepper. Form meat into 2 large patties, 1 to 1 & 1/2 inches thick. Drizzle patties with evoo. Cook 5 minutes on each side for medium-rare, 8 minutes on each side for medium-well.

Toast rolls under hot broiler or in toaster oven. Spread pâté on bun bottoms. Top with burger, cornichons, and lettuce. Spread bun tops with mustard and set on burgers. Serve with green salad and chips.

RACHAEL RAY

TOP 30

30-MINUTE MEALS

PECAN-CRUSTED CHICKEN TENDERS

SALAD *with* TANGY MAPLE BARBECUE DRESSING

CHEDDAR & CHIVE BREAD

makes 4 to 6 servings

PECAN-CRUSTED CHICKEN TENDERS *and* Salad with Tangy Maple Barbecue Dressing

Vegetable oil, for frying

1 & 1/3 to 2 pounds chicken tenders

Salt and freshly ground black pepper, to taste

1 cup all-purpose flour

2 eggs, beaten with a splash of milk or water

1 cup plain bread crumbs

1 cup pecans, finely chopped in a food processor

1/2 teaspoon nutmeg, freshly grated or ground

The zest of 1 orange

Dressing:

1/4 cup maple syrup

1/4 cup tangy barbecue sauce

The juice of 1 navel orange

1/4 cup extra-virgin olive oil

Salad:

3 hearts of romaine lettuce, shredded

6 radishes, thinly sliced

6 scallions, trimmed and chopped on an angle

Salt and freshly ground black pepper, to taste

Heat 1 & 1/2 to 2 inches oil over medium-high heat in a skillet.

Season chicken with salt and pepper. Set out 3 shallow dishes. Place flour in one, eggs beaten with water or milk in a second. In the third dish, combine bread crumbs with ground pecans, nutmeg, and orange zest. Coat tenders in batches in flour, then egg, then bread crumbs and pecans. Fry tenders in small batches, 6 to 7 minutes, and drain them on paper towels.

For dressing, combine maple syrup, barbecue sauce and orange juice in a bowl. Whisk in oil, and set aside while cooking the chicken tenders.

Combine romaine, radishes, and scallions in a large salad bowl. Toss with 3/4 of the dressing. Season with salt and pepper, to taste. Top with pecan-crusted chicken tenders and drizzle remaining dressing over top.

"Cooking is more art than science. Your most important instruments are your hands and your palate—learn to trust them.**"**

CHEDDAR & CHIVE BREAD

1 loaf baguette or French bread, split lengthwise, then
   cut in half
2 cups shredded sharp cheddar cheese
10 blades fresh chives, chopped

Heat broiler. Lightly toast bread under hot broiler. Remove
and cover with shredded cheddar cheese. Sprinkle
chopped chives liberally on top and set aside. When
ready to serve your meal, return bread to broiler. When
cheese is bubbly and lightly browned, remove from broiler
and cut into 2-inch slices or large cubes. Use as an alter-
native to croutons, when needed.

◆ ◆ ◆ ◆ ◆ **12** ◆ ◆ ◆ ◆ ◆

RACHAEL RAY

30-MINUTE MEALS

JOHN'S HADDOCK
with BACON, ONIONS AND TOMATOES

WILTED SPINACH
with BUTTER & WINE

makes 2 servings

John's **HADDOCK**

with **Bacon, Onions, and Tomatoes**

1 pound haddock fillet, cut into two portions

1 tablespoon lemon juice

Salt

Extra-virgin olive oil, for drizzling

1/2 tablespoon butter, softened

3 slices smoky bacon, chopped

3 or 4 cippolini, peeled and thinly sliced or a small to medium yellow onion, quartered then thinly sliced

1/2 cup Italian bread crumbs

2 to 3 tablespoons chopped fresh flat-leaf parsley

1 plum tomato, seeded and chopped

Preheat the oven to 400°F.

Rinse fish and pat dry. Sprinkle fish with lemon juice and salt. Coat an oven-safe skillet with a drizzle of evoo and the softened butter. Set fish into skillet. If your skillet doesn't have an oven-safe handle, wrap it in tin foil twice and it should be fine in oven.

Heat a small skillet over medium-high heat. Add a drizzle of evoo and the bacon. Render the bacon fat 3 minutes, then add onions. Cook onions until soft, 5 minutes. Remove pan from heat. Add bread crumbs to the pan and turn to coat them in drippings. Add parsley and com-

"When it comes to lighting, candles are an inexpensive cure-all."

bine. Top fish with coating of bread crumb mixture. Bake 15 minutes. Transfer fish to dinner plates, top with chopped tomato, and serve.

WILTED SPINACH
with Butter & Wine

2 tablespoons butter, cut into small pieces

1 sack (1 pound) triple-washed spinach, tough stems removed and coarsely chopped

1/2 cup dry white wine

Salt and freshly ground black pepper, to taste

Heat a medium skillet over medium heat. Melt butter into pan. Add spinach in bunches, adding more as it wilts down. When all is wilted, add wine and turn to coat. Let wine cook down a minute or two. Season with salt and pepper and serve.

RACHAEL RAY

TOP 30

30-MINUTE MEALS

STEAK
au POIVRE

ARUGULA-STUFFED
TOMATOES

makes 4 servings

STEAK AU POIVRE
and Arugula-Stuffed Tomatoes

<u>Tomatoes:</u>

4 vine-ripe tomatoes, red or yellow, tops trimmed and
seeded

Extra-virgin olive oil, for drizzling

Salt and freshly ground black pepper, to taste

<u>Stuffing:</u>

1/2 cup bread crumbs or 1 slice (1/2-inch thick) stale
crusty bread, torn

1/2 cup grated Parmigiano Reggiano cheese

1/2 teaspoon crushed red pepper flakes

1 clove garlic, chopped

2 cups arugula leaves

1 tablespoon extra-virgin olive oil

<u>Steaks:</u>

4 New York strip steaks, 1-inch thick

3 tablespoons coarsely ground black pepper

Olive oil to coat skillet

1/4 cup good brandy

2 tablespoons butter

Remove steaks from refrigerator and allow them to come to room temperature for about 10 minutes.

Preheat oven to 400°F.

Arrange tomatoes on broiler pan and drizzle with oil and season with salt and pepper. Combine bread crumbs, cheese, red pepper flakes, garlic, arugula, and 1 table-spoon oil in food processor. Pulse grind to form stuffing. Stuff tomatoes to the rims with mixture and place on center rack of oven. Bake 10 to 12 minutes. Let stand 5 minutes before serving.

Place a heavy-bottomed skillet over medium-high to high heat. Coat steaks liberally on both sides with coarse black pepper. To a very hot pan, drizzle oil to thinly coat the cooking surface. It will smoke. Add steaks immediately. Sear and seal the steaks, cooking them 4 minutes on each side, for medium-rare. For medium to medium-well, reduce heat a bit and cook 5 minutes longer. Remove steaks and let stand 5 minutes. Add brandy to the skillet and warm, then ignite, using a wooden match. Stand back. Let flames burn off, then add butter. Spoon pan juices over steaks. Serve alongside stuffed tomatoes.

RACHAEL RAY

TOP 30

30-MINUTE MEALS

CUBANO BURGERS

MANGO-BLACK BEAN SALSA

SERVE *with* PLANTAIN CHIPS

makes 4 servings

CUBANO BURGERS
with **Mango–Black Bean Salsa**

<u>Burgers:</u>
1 & 1/3 pounds ground turkey breast
1/3 pound deli-sliced smoked ham, chopped
2 cloves garlic, minced
1/4 red bell pepper, finely chopped
3 scallions, finely chopped
2 tablespoons chopped fresh cilantro
1 tablespoon Montreal Steak Seasoning by McCormick
Vegetable oil or olive oil, for drizzling
8 deli slices (1/3 pound) Swiss cheese
4 Portuguese or crusty Kaiser rolls, split
2 large dill pickles, thinly sliced lengthwise
Sliced banana pepper rings, drained
Yellow mustard

<u>Salsa:</u>
1 jar (16 ounces) black bean salsa
1 ripe mango, peeled and diced
2 tablespoons chopped fresh cilantro
1/4 red bell pepper, finely chopped

"When you eat well, you get to eat more."

Make the burgers: Place turkey in a mixing bowl and add ham, garlic, red bell pepper, scallions, cilantro, and grill seasoning; combine. Form mixture into 4 large patties; drizzle patties with oil.

Heat a large nonstick skillet over medium-high heat. Cook patties until done, 5 to 6 minutes on each side, topping each patty with 2 slices Swiss cheese in the last 2 minutes of cooking time.

Place burgers on bun bottoms and top with sliced dill pickles and banana peppers. Transfer salsa to a serving bowl and top with mango, cilantro, and red bell pepper. Slather the bun tops with mustard and set in place. Serve burgers with plantain chips, and pass salsa for dipping chips or to top burgers.

RACHAEL RAY

TOP 30

30-MINUTE MEALS

GRILLED HALIBUT TACOS
with GUACAMOLE SAUCE

CORN ON THE COB
with CHILI AND LIME

makes 4 servings

GRILLED HALIBUT TACOS
with Guacamole Sauce

4 pieces fresh halibut, steak or fillets (6 to 8 ounces each)

Extra-virgin olive oil, for drizzling

Salt and freshly ground black pepper

The juice of 1 lime

3 small to medium ripe Haas avocados, pitted and
   scooped from skins with a large spoon

The juice of 1 lemon

1/4 teaspoon cayenne pepper

1 cup plain yogurt

1 teaspoon coarse salt

2 plum tomatoes, seeded and chopped

2 scallions, thinly sliced on an angle

1 heart romaine lettuce

12 soft tortillas (6-inch)

Preheat a grill pan or indoor grill to high setting or prepare
outdoor grill. Drizzle halibut on both sides with olive oil.
Season with salt and pepper, to taste. Grill fish, 5 to 6
minutes on each side, or until opaque. Squeeze lime
juice over the fish and remove from the pan or grill. Flake
fish into large chunks with a fork.

While fish is cooking, combine avocado, lemon juice,

cayenne pepper, yogurt, and salt in a blender or food processor. Process until smooth. Remove guacamole to a bowl and stir in tomatoes and scallions. Shred lettuce and reserve.

When fish comes off the grill pan or grill, blister and heat the tortillas. To assemble, pile some of the fish chunks onto tortillas and slather with guacamole sauce. Top with shredded lettuce, fold tacos over and eat!

CORN ON THE COB
with Chili and Lime

4 ears sweet corn, shucked and cleaned
1 lime, cut into wedges
1/3 stick butter, cut into pats
Chili powder, for sprinkling
Salt, to taste

In a medium pot, bring water to a boil and simmer corn, 3 to 5 minutes. Drain and arrange on a plate in a single row. Squeeze lime juice liberally over the ears. Nest pats of butter into paper towels and rub the corn with butter. Season with a sprinkle of chili powder and salt, and serve immediately.

RACHAEL RAY

TOP 30

30-MINUTE MEALS

TUNA STEAK *au* POIVRE

WHITE BEANS *with* ROSEMARY & ROASTED RED PEPPERS

makes 4 servings

TUNA STEAK AU POIVRE
on White Beans with Rosemary & Roasted Red Peppers

4 tuna steaks, 1 & 1/2 inches thick (6 ounces each)

Coarse salt

Extra-virgin olive oil, for drizzling

Coarse freshly ground black pepper

Lemon wedges, for passing

Beans:

2 tablespoons extra-virgin olive oil

2 cloves garlic, finely chopped

1 small onion, chopped

2 cans (15 ounces each) cannellini beans, rinsed and drained

1 roasted red pepper, storebought or homemade, diced (see Note)

2 sprigs fresh rosemary, leaves stripped and finely chopped

A handful chopped fresh flat-leaf parsley

Coarse salt and freshly ground black pepper, to taste

"Beginners allowed! You can make any meal in here, that's my promise."

Preheat a large nonstick skillet or grill pan over high heat. Pat tuna steaks dry and season with a little coarse salt. Drizzle olive oil over tuna to lightly coat on both sides. Season one side of the steaks with a generous coating of coarse ground black pepper. When the pan is very hot, add steaks, peppered-side down. Sear and brown them 2 minutes, then turn and immediately reduce heat to medium. Loosely cover pan with a tin foil tent and allow steaks to cook 2 to 3 minutes for rare, 5 minutes for medium, and 7 minutes for well done.

In a second skillet over moderate heat, coat pan with olive oil, add garlic and onion and sauté, 3 minutes, to soften onion bits. Add beans and chopped roasted red pepper and heat through, 2 to 3 minutes. Stir in rosemary and parsley and season beans with salt and pepper.

Place a serving of beans on a dinner plate and top with Tuna Steak.

Note: To roast red peppers, preheat broiler to high. Halve and seed pepper and place skin-side-up close to hot broiler to blacken skins. Transfer pepper to a brown paper sack and seal to keep in the steam. When cool enough to handle, peel away charred skins.

RACHAEL RAY

TOP 30

30-MINUTE MEALS

URBAN COWBOY
TURKEY BURGERS

SPICY "O-NUTS"

makes 4 servings

Urban Cowboy
TURKEY BURGERS

8 slices turkey or applewood-smoked bacon

1 & 1/3 pounds ground turkey breast

2 cloves garlic, finely chopped

1 large shallot or 1/4 red onion, finely chopped

2 tablespoons chopped fresh thyme or 1 teaspoon dried

2 tablespoons chopped fresh cilantro or parsley

1/2 small green, red, or yellow bell pepper, seeded and finely chopped

1 serrano or jalapeño pepper, seeded and finely chopped

2 teaspoons ground cumin

1 to 2 teaspoons hot sauce, such as Tabasco

2 teaspoons Montreal Steak Seasoning by McCormick

Vegetable oil or olive oil, for drizzling

1/2 pound deli-sliced pepper-Jack cheese

4 crusty Kaiser rolls, split

1 cup sweet red pepper relish or pepper jelly

Red leaf lettuce

Heat a large nonstick skillet over medium-high heat; cook bacon until crisp. Remove bacon, wipe excess grease from skillet, and return skillet to heat.

While bacon is cooking, combine turkey, garlic, shallot or onion, thyme, cilantro or parsley, bell pepper, serrano or jalapeño pepper, cumin, hot sauce, and grill seasoning. Divide mixture into 4 equal mounds then form into patties. Drizzle patties with vegetable oil to coat. Cook in skillet over medium-high heat until done, 5 to 6 minutes on each side, placing sliced cheese over the patties in the last 2 minutes of cooking.

Place cooked cheeseburgers on buns. Spread sweet relish on bun tops and set lettuce into place using relish as "glue." Top cheeseburgers with 2 slices bacon, then serve.

"No fancy equipment or hard-to-find ingredients required.**"**

SPICY "O-NUTS"

Vegetable oil, for frying

1 extra-large sweet onion, peeled, sliced, and
separated into 3/4-inch-thick rings

2 cups complete pancake mix

1 bottle (12 ounces) cold beer

1 teaspoon sweet paprika

2 teaspoons chili powder

1 tablespoon hot sauce, such as Tabasco

Salt, to taste

Pour 1 inch vegetable oil into a large skillet over medium-high heat. To test the oil, add a 1-inch cube of bread to hot oil; if it turns deep golden brown in a count to 40, the oil is ready.

Place 1/4 cup pancake mix in a resealable bag and add onion rings. Toss to coat onion rings.

Mix together the remaining 1 & 3/4 cups pancake mix, beer, paprika, chili powder, and hot sauce. Working in batches of 5 to 6 slices, coat onion rings in batter and fry until evenly golden brown, 4 to 5 minutes. Transfer to paper towels to drain. Season o-nuts with salt while hot. Repeat with remaining onions. When all the onions are dipped and fried, turn off oil to cool before discarding. Serve o-nuts hot.

RACHAEL RAY
TOP 30
30-MINUTE MEALS

MARINATED GRILLED FLANK STEAK

BLT-SMASHED POTATOES

SERVE *with* STEAMED VEGETABLES

makes 2 servings

Marinated **GRILLED FLANK STEAK** *with* BLT–Smashed Potatoes

2 cloves garlic, finely chopped

1 tablespoon Montreal Steak Seasoning by McCormick

1 teaspoon smoked paprika, chili powder, ground cumin, or ground chipotles

2 teaspoons hot sauce, such as Tabasco

1 tablespoon Worcestershire sauce

2 tablespoons red wine vinegar (2 splashes)

1/3 cup extra-virgin olive oil, plus a drizzle

1 & 1/2 pounds flank steak

1 & 1/2 pounds small new red-skinned potatoes

1 leek, trimmed of tough tops

4 slices thick-cut smoky bacon, such as applewood-smoked, chopped

1 small can (15 ounces) diced tomatoes, well-drained

1/2 cup sour cream, half-and-half, or chicken broth

Salt and freshly ground black pepper, to taste

Mix garlic, grill seasoning, paprika, hot sauce, Worcestershire sauce, vinegar, and 1/3 cup evoo in a shallow dish. Place meat in marinade and coat evenly. Let stand 15 minutes.

Meanwhile, cut larger potatoes in half; leave small ones

"Surprise a few friends with a weeknight invitation—watch a game or just hang out.**"**

whole. Place potatoes in a small pot and cover with water. Cover pot. Bring to a boil, remove lid, then cook until tender, 12 to 15 minutes.

Heat a grill pan or cast-iron pan over high heat.

Cut leek in half lengthwise. Chop into 1/2-inch pieces. Place in a bowl of water and swish, separating the layers, to release the dirt. Drain in a colander or strainer.

Grill flank steak in hot pan; 4 minutes on each side for medium rare to medium, and 6 or 7 minutes for medium-well.

Heat a small skillet over medium-high heat. Add a drizzle of evoo and the bacon. Cook until it begins to crisp and has rendered most of its fat, 3 to 5 minutes. Add leeks and cook until tender, 2 to 3 minutes. Add tomatoes and heat, 1 minute.

Drain potatoes and return them to the hot pot. Smash potatoes with sour cream, half-and-half, or chicken broth and the BLT: bacon, leeks, and tomatoes. Season with salt and pepper.

Remove steak from grill and let it sit a few minutes before slicing. Thinly slice meat on an angle, cutting against the grain. Serve with BLT potatoes and a side of steamed vegetables.

RACHAEL RAY

TOP 30

30-MINUTE MEALS

YOU-WON'T-BE-SINGLE-FOR-LONG VODKA CREAM PASTA

HEART-Y SALAD: HEARTS OF ROMAINE, PALM & ARTICHOKE

makes 2 servings

(with some leftovers)

You-Won't-Be-Single-For-Long
VODKA CREAM PASTA

1 tablespoon extra-virgin olive oil

1 tablespoon butter

2 garlic cloves, minced

2 shallots, minced

1 cup vodka

1 cup chicken stock

1 can (28 ounces) crushed tomatoes

Coarse salt and freshly ground black pepper, to taste

1/2 cup heavy cream

12 ounces pasta, such as penne rigate

20 leaves fresh basil, shredded or torn

Crusty bread

Put large pot of salted water on to boil.

Heat a large skillet over moderate heat. Add oil, butter, garlic, and shallots. Gently sauté garlic and shallots, 3 to 5 minutes. Add vodka, about 3 turns around the pan in a steady stream. Reduce vodka by half, 2 or 3 minutes. Add chicken stock and tomatoes. Bring sauce to a bubble, then reduce heat to simmer. Season with salt and pepper.

While sauce simmers, cook pasta in salted boiling water

until al dente. While pasta cooks, prepare the salad.

Stir cream into vodka sauce. When sauce returns to a bubble, remove from heat. Drain pasta. Toss hot pasta with sauce and basil leaves. Serve immediately, with crusty bread.

HEART-Y SALAD: Hearts of Romaine, Palm & Artichoke

1 heart romaine lettuce, shredded
1 cup fresh flat-leaf parsley leaves (half a bundle)
1 can (14 ounces), hearts of palm, drained
1/4 pound prosciutto di Parma
1 can (15 ounces) quartered artichoke hearts in water, drained
1/4 pound wedge Pecorino, Romano or Asiago cheese
Balsamic vinegar and extra-virgin olive oil, for drizzling
Salt and freshly ground black pepper, to taste

Place romaine on a platter and toss with parsley. Wrap hearts of palm in prosciutto and cut into bite-size pieces on an angle. Arrange palm and artichoke over the romaine. Shave cheese with a vegetable peeler into short ribbons, working over the salad plate. Drizzle with vinegar and oil; season with salt and pepper.

RACHAEL RAY

TOP 30

30-MINUTE MEALS

SWEET 'N SPICY
CHICKEN CURRY IN A HURRY WITH
FRAGRANT BASMATI RICE

makes 4 servings

◆ ◆ ◆ ◆ ◆ **20** ◆ ◆ ◆ ◆ ◆

Sweet 'n Spicy
CHICKEN CURRY IN A HURRY
with Fragrant Basmati Rice

2 cups basmati rice

1 teaspoon each coriander seeds, cumin seeds,
  mustard seeds (optional)

2 tablespoons vegetable or canola oil

1 & 1/3 to 1 & 1/2 pounds chicken tenders, diced

2 to 4 cloves garlic, minced (to your taste)

1 to 2 inches fresh gingerroot, minced or grated
  (to your taste)

1 large yellow onion, chopped

1 can chicken broth (about 2 cups)

2 tablespoons curry paste, mild or hot

1 cup mincemeat (found on the baking aisle)

Coarse salt, to taste

Toppings and garnishes (mix and match):

4 scallions, chopped

1 cup toasted coconut

1/2 cup sliced almonds or Spanish peanuts

1 cup prepared mango chutney

1/4 cup cilantro finely chopped

91

"Make your own take-out. In as much time as it takes for delivery, you'll have fresh, good-for-you-food."

For spicy rice, toast coriander, cumin, and mustard seeds in the bottom of a medium saucepan. When seeds pop and become fragrant, add water, bring to a boil, and prepare rice according to package directions. For plain rice, prepare as usual.

Heat oil in a large, deep, nonstick skillet over medium-high heat. Add chicken and lightly brown. Add garlic, ginger, and onion, and sauté another 5 minutes. Add chicken broth and bring to a bubble. Stir in curry paste and mincemeat and reduce heat to medium low. Add salt to taste. Simmer, 5 to 10 minutes.

Assemble toppings in small dishes. Serve chicken curry in shallow bowls with scoops of plain or spiced basmati rice. Garnish with your choice of toppings.

RACHAEL RAY

TOP 30

30-MINUTE MEALS

PORTOBELLO BURGERS *with* ROASTED PEPPER SPREAD

SERVE *with* FANCY CHIPS *and* CHUNKED VEGETABLE SALAD

makes 4 "Burgers"

PORTOBELLO BURGERS
with Roasted Pepper Spread

4 medium portobello mushroom caps

Marinade:

3 splashes balsamic vinegar (2 to 3 tablespoons)

3 tablespoons extra-virgin olive oil

4 or 5 dashes Worcestershire sauce

2 sprigs fresh rosemary, leaves stripped from stem, minced

Montreal Steak Seasoning by McCormick or coarse salt
   and black pepper, to taste

4 thin slices provolone cheese, or fresh smoked
   mozzarella

Spread:

1 jar (14 ounces) roasted red pepper, drained, or 3
   homemade roasted peppers

1 clove garlic, cracked from skin

A drizzle extra-virgin olive oil

A handful fresh flat-leaf parsley

A pinch coarse salt and black pepper, to taste

4 pieces Romaine lettuce or arugula

4 thin slices red onion (optional)

4 crusty Kaiser or Italian hard rolls, split and toasted

Quickly rinse and pat dry caps, set aside. Combine marinade, except Montreal Seasoning, in a large plastic food storage bag. Add mushroom caps, seal, and shake to evenly coat.

Heat a nonstick griddle or skillet over medium-high heat. Add portobellos and cook, 3 to 5 minutes on each side, turning once. Season each side with a little steak seasoning or salt and pepper as they cook. Caps should be tender and dark when done. Place a slice of cheese on each cap and remove from heat.

Combine ingredients for the roasted red pepper spread in a food processor and pulse until a paste is formed.

Toast rolls lightly under broiler or toaster oven. Spread generously with roasted pepper. Pile "burgers" in this order: bottom of roll, Portobello with cheese, Romaine or arugula leaves, red onion slice, and roll top. Garnish with fancy chips, such as Yukon Gold onion and garlic chips by Terra brand, and a nice chunked vegetable salad.

RACHAEL RAY

TOP 30

30-MINUTE MEALS

STEAK PIZZAOLA
with THE WORKS

ROMAINE SALAD *with*
BLUE CHEESE VINAIGRETTE

makes 2 BIG GUY servings

STEAK PIZZAOLA *with* The Works

1 & 1/2 to 2 pounds porterhouse or rib-eye steak
Salt and freshly ground black pepper
3 tablespoons extra-virgin olive oil
4 cloves garlic, cracked away from the skin
1 teaspoon crushed red pepper flakes
12 mushrooms, sliced
1 small onion, sliced
1 green bell pepper, seeded and sliced
1/3 stick pepperoni, casing removed, chopped (optional)
1/2 cup dry red wine
1 can (28 ounces) crushed tomatoes
1 teaspoon dried oregano or 2 teaspoons chopped fresh
1/4 cup grated Parmigiano Reggiano or Romano cheese

Heat a large nonstick skillet over high heat. Season the steak with salt and pepper. Add 2 tablespoons evoo to the pan, then steak. Brown 3 minutes on each side and remove. Add remaining tablespoon of evoo to pan and reduce heat to medium-high. Add garlic, pepper flakes, mushrooms, onions, bell peppers, and pepperoni, if using. Cook 5 minutes, then add wine and scrape up bits. Add tomatoes, oregano, and salt and pepper to

"Have fun in the kitchen."

taste. Slide steak back in and reduce heat to medium. Cover pan and cook 5 or 6 minutes for medium rare, 10 to 12 minutes for medium well. Remove meat; cut away from bone or divide into 2 large portions. Cover steaks with sauce and top with grated cheese.

ROMAINE SALAD
with Blue Cheese Vinaigrette

2 hearts romaine, chopped

1 clove garlic, chopped

1/2 teaspoon dried oregano

2 teaspoons sugar

2 tablespoons red wine vinegar

1/4 cup extra-virgin olive oil

1/4 pound blue cheese crumbles

Salt and freshly ground black pepper, to taste

Place romaine in a big bowl. In a small bowl, combine garlic, oregano, sugar, and vinegar. Add evoo to dressing in a slow stream and mix with a whisk or fork. Stir in blue cheese. Pour dressing over salad and toss. Season with salt and pepper, and serve.

◆ ◆ ◆ ◆ ◆ **23** ◆ ◆ ◆ ◆ ◆

RACHAEL RAY

TOP 30

30-MINUTE MEALS

CAESAR SALAD
THE REAL DEAL, YES, YOU HAVE
TO USE AN EGG,
NO MUSTARD, HOLD THE MAYO

MARK ANTONY'S SCAMPI TOPPING

makes 2 servings

102

CAESAR SALAD The Real Deal, Yes, You Have to Use an Egg, No Mustard, Hold the Mayo

<u>Croutons:</u>

1 clove garlic

Extra-virgin olive oil

8 to 10 large cubes chewy bread

<u>Salad:</u>

2 large cloves garlic

2 anchovy fillets, plus extra for garnish

1/3 cup extra-virgin olive oil

1 egg yolk (see Note)

4 shakes Worcestershire sauce

1 lemon

3 hearts romaine lettuce

A handful grated Parmigiano Reggiano cheese, plus extra shavings for the table

Cracked black pepper, to taste

Pop a clove of garlic from its skin with a whack using the flat of your knife. Rub the surface of a heavy-bottomed skillet with the cracked clove. Leaving the clove in the skillet, place over medium-low heat and coat the bottom with a thin layer of olive oil. Add the bread. Let it hang out, giving the pan a shake now and then, for 20 minutes, or until cubes are golden brown.

Rub the sides and bottom of your salad bowl, all the better if it's wooden, with the two garlic cloves you'll use in the dressing. After rubbing the bowl, place the garlic pieces, anchovies, and olive oil in a small saucepan. Heat over medium heat until anchovies melt completely into the oil; their fishy flavor will not be distinguishable—just a nice, subtle, salty but almost nutty presence will remain. Remove the garlic and discard. (The oil will be infused with the flavor.) Pour the oil into the bottom of the salad bowl. Separate the egg. Discard the white. Mix yolk into oil with a fork. Add Worcestershire. Roll lemon on counter to release juices. Cut lemon in half and squeeze juice into bowl. Mix vigorously with fork. Coarsely chop the lettuce hearts and dump into bowl. Add cheese, a lot of pepper, and croutons. Coat the salad completely, tossing and turning several times. Serve with extra cheese and pepper.

Note: If you're worried about the raw egg, use a splash of pasteurized egg product.

"When a special occasion comes up, why not choose to stay in—in style!"

Mark Antony's
SCAMPI TOPPING

2 cloves garlic, minced
A pinch crushed red pepper flakes
2 tablespoons extra-virgin olive oil
10 jumbo shrimp, peeled and deveined
A shot white wine

Heat garlic and crushed red pepper in oil over medium-high heat until the garlic speaks. Add shrimp and cook for a minute on each side, keeping pan moving with vigorous shakes to avoid burning garlic. Douse with a little white wine and serve on top of Caesar greens.

RACHAEL RAY

TOP 30

30-MINUTE MEALS

CHICKEN PICCATA PASTA TOSS

EMMANUEL'S BAKED ARTICHOKE HEARTS

makes 4 servings

Emmanuel's Baked
ARTICHOKE HEARTS

2 cans (15 ounces each) artichoke hearts in water, 6 to
   8 count, drained
1 tablespoon extra-virgin olive oil, plus a drizzle for
   baking dish
The juice of 1/4 lemon
1 tablespoon butter
3 cloves garlic, chopped
6 anchovy fillets
1 cup Italian-style bread crumbs (3 handfuls)
1/4 cup chopped fresh flat-leaf parsley
1/4 cup grated Parmigiano Reggiano
Coarse freshly ground black pepper

Preheat oven to 400°F.

Turn artichokes upside down to get all the liquid out, and
cut them in half lengthwise. Drizzle a small casserole dish
with a little olive oil, spreading it with a pastry brush.
Arrange artichokes with tops up, bottoms down, in a lay-
ered pattern in the dish. Top with lemon juice.

Preheat a small nonstick skillet over medium heat. Add oil
and butter to the skillet. When the butter melts into the
oil, add garlic and anchovies. Using the back of a wood-
en spoon, work the anchovies into the oil as they break

up. When anchovies have dissolved, add bread crumbs and lightly toast, about 2 to 3 minutes. Add parsley, cheese, and pepper, stir to combine and remove from heat. Top artichokes with an even layer of bread topping and set in the middle of oven. Bake until topping is deep golden brown, about 10 minutes.

CHICKEN PICCATA Pasta Toss

1 pound penne rigate pasta, cooked al dente

2 tablespoons extra-virgin olive oil

1 & 1/4 pounds chicken tenders, cut into 1-inch pieces

Salt and freshly ground black pepper, to taste

2 tablespoons butter

4 cloves garlic, chopped

2 medium shallots, chopped

2 tablespoons flour

1/2 cup white wine

The juice of 1 lemon

1 cup chicken broth or stock

3 tablespoons capers, drained

1/2 cup chopped fresh flat-leaf parsley

Chopped or snipped chives, for garnish

Heat a deep nonstick skillet over medium-high heat. Add 1 tablespoon of olive oil and the chicken to the pan. Season with salt and pepper, and brown until lightly golden, about 5 to 6 minutes. Remove chicken from pan and set it in your serving dish while you complete the sauce.

Return the skillet to the heat, reduced to medium. To the skillet, add another tablespoon olive oil, 1 tablespoon butter, the garlic and the shallots and sauté, 3 minutes. Stir in flour and cook, 2 minutes. Whisk in wine and reduce liquid, 1 minute. Whisk lemon juice and broth into sauce. Stir in capers and parsley. When sauce comes to a bubble, add remaining tablespoon butter to give it a little shine.

Put chicken back in the pan and heat through a minute or two. Toss hot pasta with chicken and sauce. Adjust salt and pepper to taste. Top with fresh snipped chives and serve.

RACHAEL RAY

TOP 30

30-MINUTE MEALS

BARBECUE SAUCY SALMON

ROMAINE SALAD *with* ORANGE VINAIGRETTE

makes 2 servings

Barbecue Saucy SALMON *on* Romaine Salad with Orange Vinaigrette

Salmon and Barbecue Glaze:

1 tablespoon extra-virgin olive oil, plus a little for drizzling

1/4 red onion, finely chopped

2 tablespoons red wine vinegar

1/2 cup maple syrup

1 tablespoon tomato paste

2 teaspoons Worcestershire sauce

1 teaspoon curry powder

2 to 3 drops Liquid Smoke

1/2 teaspoon freshly ground black pepper

2 salmon fillets or salmon steaks (6 to 8 ounces each)

Salt

Salad and Dressing:

The zest and juice of 1 small navel orange

1 clove garlic, finely chopped

2 teaspoons Dijon mustard

2 tablespoons chopped fresh tarragon or 1 teaspoon dried

1 teaspoon salt

1/4 cup extra-virgin olive oil

2 hearts romaine lettuce

3 scallions, chopped

Make the glaze: Heat a small saucepan over medium heat, add evoo then onion, and cook onion 3 minutes. Add vinegar and cook until reduced by half. Add syrup, tomato paste, Worcestershire, curry, Liquid Smoke, and pepper. Bring to a bubble and simmer.

Meanwhile, start the salmon: Heat a grill pan over medium-high heat. Drizzle salmon with evoo and season with salt. Grill for 3 minutes and baste liberally with the glaze. Flip salmon and glaze opposite side. If you like your salmon pink at the center, remove after another 3 minutes; for opaque salmon, grill 5 minutes on each side.

Make the salad: Whisk orange zest and juice with garlic, Dijon, tarragon, and salt, then stream in evoo, whisking to combine. Chop lettuce and toss with scallions and dressing. Pile salad onto plates and top with glazed barbecued salmon.

RACHAEL RAY

TOP 30

30-MINUTE MEALS

DELMONICO STEAKS *with* BALSAMIC ONIONS *and* STEAK SAUCE

BLUE CHEESE & WALNUT SPINACH SALAD *with* MAPLE DRESSING

makes 4 servings

DELMONICO STEAKS
with Balsamic Onions and Steak Sauce

4 Delmonico steaks, 1-inch thick (10 to 12 ounces each)

2 teaspoons extra-virgin olive oil

Montreal Steak Seasoning by McCormick or coarse salt and black pepper, to taste

Onions:

1 tablespoon extra-virgin olive oil

2 large yellow onions, thinly sliced

1/4 cup balsamic vinegar

Steak Sauce:

1 & 1/2 teaspoons extra-virgin olive oil

2 cloves garlic, chopped

1 small white boiling onion, chopped

1/4 cup dry cooking sherry

1 cup canned tomato sauce

1 tablespoon Worcestershire sauce

Freshly ground black pepper, to taste

Heat a heavy grill pan or griddle pan over high heat, and wipe it with olive oil using tongs and a paper towel. Cook steaks 4 minutes on each side for medium, 7 to 8 minutes for medium well. Season with steak seasoning or salt and pepper and remove to a warm platter.

Onions: Heat a medium nonstick skillet over medium-high heat. Add oil and sliced yellow onions and cook, stirring occasionally, 10 to 12 minutes, until onions are soft and sweet. Add balsamic vinegar to the pan and turn onions until vinegar cooks away and glazes onions a deep brown, 3 to 5 minutes.

Steak Sauce: Heat a small saucepan over medium heat. Add oil, garlic and white onions and sauté, 5 minutes until tender. Add sherry to the pan and combine with onions. Stir in tomato sauce and Worcestershire and season with black pepper.

To serve, top steaks with onions and drizzle a little steak sauce down over the top, reserving half to pass at table.

Blue Cheese & Walnut SPINACH SALAD *with* Maple Dressing

1 sack (10 ounces) baby spinach
1/3 pound blue cheese, crumbled
1 can (6 ounces) walnut halves, toasted
1/4 cup maple syrup, warmed
1 & 1/2 tablespoons cider vinegar
1/4 cup extra-virgin olive oil
Salt and freshly ground black pepper

Place spinach on a large platter. Top with blue cheese and walnuts. Warm maple syrup in a small saucepan. Pour vinegar into a small bowl. Whisk oil into vinegar in a slow stream, then whisk in maple syrup slowly. Pour dressing over the salad and serve. Season with salt and pepper, to taste.

RACHAEL RAY

TOP 30

30-MINUTE MEALS

SAGE VEAL CHOPS

ARUGULA SALAD
with **BLUE CHEESE, PEARS,
AND APRICOT VINAIGRETTE**

makes 4 servings

SAGE VEAL CHOPS

4 veal chops, 1-inch thick

Salt and freshly ground black pepper, to taste

6 sprigs fresh sage, chopped (about 4 tablespoons)

1 tablespoon extra-virgin olive oil

2 tablespoons butter

1/2 cup dry white wine

Heat a heavy-bottomed skillet over medium-high heat. Season chops with salt and pepper and rub them each with about 1 tablespoon of chopped sage, rubbing well into both sides of the chops. Add oil to the pan. Melt butter into the oil and add chops to the pan. Cook 5 minutes on each side, remove to warm platter, and let rest. Add wine to the pan and scrape up the drippings. Spoon over the chops and serve.

ARUGULA SALAD *with* Blue Cheese, Pears, and Apricot Vinaigrette

2 bunches arugula, washed and dried, stems trimmed
1 head Bibb lettuce, torn
The juice of 1/2 lemon
1 ripe pear, thinly sliced
1/2 pound Maytag or other blue cheese, crumbled

<u>Dressing:</u>
1 small shallot, minced
2 tablespoons white wine vinegar
1/4 cup apricot all-fruit spread
1/3 cup extra-virgin olive oil
Salt and freshly ground black pepper, to taste

Combine arugula and lettuce in a salad bowl. Squeeze a little lemon juice over pear slices to keep them from browning. Arrange them on top of the lettuce and arugula. Top with blue cheese crumbles.

To make the dressing, combine shallots, vinegar, and apricot spread in a bowl. Stream in oil as you whisk. Add to salad, season with salt and black pepper and serve.

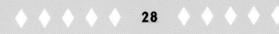

RACHAEL RAY

TOP 30

30-MINUTE MEALS

TUNA BURGERS
with GINGER AND SOY

GRILLED RED ONIONS

SERVE *with*
ROOT VEGETABLE CHIPS
and PICKLED GINGER

makes 4 servings

GUY*food*

TUNA BURGERS
with Ginger and Soy

1 & 1/2 pounds fresh tuna steak

2 cloves garlic, chopped

2 inches fresh gingerroot, minced or grated

3 tablespoons Tamari (dark soy sauce)

2 scallions, chopped

1/2 small red bell pepper, finely chopped

2 teaspoons sesame oil

2 teaspoons Montreal Steak Seasoning by McCormick, or 1 teaspoon freshly ground black pepper, and 1/2 teaspoon of salt

1 tablespoon light-colored oil, such as canola or vegetable

1/2 pound shiitake mushrooms, coarsely chopped

Coarse salt, to taste

4 sesame Kaiser rolls

1 jar (8 ounces) mango chutney

4 leaves red leaf lettuce

1 jar (8 ounces) wasabi or Asian sweet hot mustard

Pickled ginger, for garnish (optional)

Preheat a nonstick griddle or a grill pan to medium-high to high heat. Cube tuna into bite-size pieces and place in a food processor. Pulse the processor to grind the tuna until it has the consistency of ground beef. Transfer to a bowl. Combine ground tuna with garlic, ginger, soy sauce, scallions, red bell pepper, sesame oil, and Montreal Seasoning or salt and black pepper. Form 4 large patties, 1 & 1/2 inches thick. Drizzle patties on both sides with oil.

Cook tuna burgers 2 to 3 minutes on each side for rare, up to 6 minutes each side for well done.

In a medium nonstick skillet over medium-high heat, sauté fresh shiitakes for 2 or 3 minutes in 1 tablespoon oil (once around the pan in a slow stream). Season mushrooms with salt and pepper.

Split the rolls and lightly toast them under broiler. Spread mango chutney on the bottom of each bun. Top with tuna burger, shiitakes, and lettuce. Spread wasabi mustard or sweet hot mustard on bun tops and set them in place. Serve with root vegetable chips and pickled ginger, if desired.

Grilled RED ONIONS

1 large red onion, unpeeled

Light-colored oil such as canola or vegetable, for drizzling

Montreal Steak Seasoning by McCormick, or coarse salt and freshly ground black pepper, to taste

Preheat a grill or nonstick griddle to hot. Trim a thin slice off the side of the unpeeled onion. Set the onion flat on the cut surface for stability. Cut the onion into 4 one-inch-thick slices. Remove the outer ring of skin from each slice. Drizzle the sliced onion with light-colored oil and season both sides with steak seasoning or salt and pepper. Grill on hot grill or on a nonstick griddle for 5 to 7 minutes on each side, until onion is tender and has begun to caramelize. Serve alongside tuna burgers.

RACHAEL RAY

TOP 30

30-MINUTE MEALS

MUSSELS *in* MEXICAN BEER

CHORIZO & SHRIMP QUESADILLAS *with* SMOKY GUACAMOLE

makes 2 servings

MUSSELS *in* **Mexican beer**

2 tablespoons extra-virgin olive oil

4 cloves garlic, cracked away from skin and crushed

1 small onion, chopped

1 jalapeño, seeded and chopped

A couple pinches salt

2 dozen mussels, scrubbed

1/2 cup dark Mexican beer, such as Negro Modelo

1 can (15 ounces), diced tomatoes, drained

2 tablespoons chopped fresh flat-leaf parsley or
  cilantro

In a deep skillet with a cover, preheated over medium-high heat, add evoo, garlic, onion, and jalapeño. Season with salt. Sauté 2 minutes. Arrange mussels in the pan. Pour in beer and tomatoes and shake the pan to combine. Cover and cook 3 to 5 minutes or until mussels open. Remove from heat and spoon sauce down into shells. Garnish with parsley or cilantro. Serve immediately from the pan.

CHORIZO & SHRIMP QUESADILLAS
with Smoky Guacamole

Guacamole:

2 ripe Haas avocados

The juice of 1 lime

A couple pinches salt

1/4 cup sour cream (3 rounded tablespoons)

2 chipotle peppers in adobo (available in cans in Mexican section of market)

Quesadillas:

1/2 pound chorizo sausage, sliced thin on an angle

1 tablespoon extra-virgin olive oil, plus some for drizzling

1 clove garlic, cracked away from skin and crushed

12 large shrimp, peeled and deveined, tails removed (ask for easy-peels at seafood counter)

Salt and freshly ground black pepper, to taste

4 twelve-inch flour tortillas

1/2 pound (2 cups) shredded pepper-Jack cheese

"The kitchen table is where it's at."

Make the guacamole: Cut avocados all the way around with a sharp knife. Scoop out pit with a spoon, then spoon out avocado flesh and place in a food processor. Add lime juice, salt, sour cream, and chipotles in adobo. Pulse until smooth. Transfer to a serving bowl.

Heat a 12-inch nonstick skillet over medium-high heat. Brown chorizo 2 to 3 minutes, then remove from pan. Add evoo and garlic, then shrimp. Season with salt and pepper, and cook shrimp until pink, 2 or 3 minutes. Transfer shrimp to a cutting board and coarsely chop.

Add a drizzle of oil to the pan, then a tortilla. Cook tortilla 30 seconds, then turn. Cover half of the tortilla with a couple handfuls of cheese. Arrange a layer of chorizo and shrimp over the cheese, and fold tortilla over. Press down gently with a spatula and cook a minute or so on each side to melt cheese, and crisp. Remove to large cutting board and repeat with remaining ingredients.

Cut each quesadilla into 5 wedges, transfer to plates, and top wedges with liberal amounts of smoky guacamole.

Make the guacamole: Cut avocados all the way around with a sharp knife. Scoop out pit with a spoon, then spoon out avocado flesh and place in a food processor. Add lime juice, salt, sour cream, and chipotles in adobo. Pulse until smooth. Transfer to a serving bowl.

Heat a 12-inch nonstick skillet over medium-high heat. Brown chorizo 2 to 3 minutes, then remove from pan. Add evoo and garlic, then shrimp. Season with salt and pepper, and cook shrimp until pink, 2 or 3 minutes. Transfer shrimp to a cutting board and coarsely chop.

Add a drizzle of oil to the pan, then a tortilla. Cook tortilla 30 seconds, then turn. Cover half of the tortilla with a couple handfuls of cheese. Arrange a layer of chorizo and shrimp over the cheese, and fold tortilla over. Press down gently with a spatula and cook a minute or so on each side to melt cheese, and crisp. Remove to large cutting board and repeat with remaining ingredients.

Cut each quesadilla into 5 wedges, transfer to plates, and top wedges with liberal amounts of smoky guacamole.

RACHAEL RAY

TOP 30

30-MINUTE MEALS

BALSAMIC PORK TENDERLOINS

ROASTED RATATOUILLE VEGETABLES

makes 4 servings

Balsamic PORK TENDERLOINS

2 pork tenderloins (2 & 1/4 pounds total)

Balsamic vinegar, for drizzling (about 3 tablespoons)

Extra-virgin olive oil, for drizzling

4 cloves garlic, cracked

2 tablespoons Montreal Steak Seasoning by McCormick
   or coarse salt and freshly ground black pepper

4 sprigs each fresh rosemary and thyme, leaves
   stripped and finely chopped

Preheat oven to 500°F.

Trim silver skin off tenderloins with a thin, very sharp knife.
Place tenderloins on a nonstick cookie sheet with a rim.
Coat tenderloins in balsamic vinegar, rubbing vinegar into
meat. Drizzle tenderloins with evoo, just enough to coat.
Cut small slits into meat and disperse chunks of cracked
garlic into meat. Combine steak seasoning blend or
coarse salt and pepper with rosemary and thyme and rub
meat with blend. Roast in hot oven 20 to 25 minutes. Let
meat rest, transfer to a carving board, slice and serve.

"A high 'can-do' attitude makes you feel like a rock star in the kitchen.**"**

30

Roasted
RATATOUILLE VEGETABLES

1 medium red bell pepper, seeded and cut lengthwise into 1-inch strips

1 medium onion, sliced

1 small eggplant, sliced into 1/2-inch pieces then piled and quartered

1 small zucchini, sliced 1/2-inch thick

2 plum tomatoes, seeded and quartered lengthwise

3 cloves garlic, crushed

Extra-virgin olive oil, to coat

2 sprigs fresh rosemary, chopped

Coarse salt and freshly ground black pepper, to taste

Preheat oven to 500°F.

Working on a cookie sheet, combine vegetables and garlic. Drizzle liberally with evoo and season with rosemary, salt, and pepper. Toss to coat vegetables evenly. Roast until just tender, 15 minutes.

Index